KENNETH M. PLUMMER

A HISTORY OF
West Virginia Wesleyan College
1890-1965

BY KENNETH M. PLUMMER

WEST VIRGINIA WESLEYAN COLLEGE PRESS
1965

A HISTORY OF
WEST VIRGINIA WESLEYAN COLLEGE
Copyright © 1965 by WEST VIRGINIA WESLEYAN COLLEGE

PRINTED BY THE PARTHENON PRESS

To

CLYDE O. LAW

1883—1964

President of the Board, 1933 to 1956

Forever a Friend

of

Wesleyan

FOREWORD

For forty years voices in the field of higher education have declared that the liberal arts college and its chief proponent, the church-related college, would soon be things of the past. The prediction of their demise has been made repeatedly over this span of years.

This history of West Virginia Wesleyan College gives the lie to prediction. Here is a lively account of how one such college has overcome a succession of difficulties to bring it to real stature in the educational world of today. In reading this book, one senses how, again and again, this college faced what would seem to be insurmountable difficulties only to prove its courage by surmounting them. Its battle to survive is heroic. The history which Professor Plummer has here written gives a clear account of the persistence that has brought this college to its present position.

Every friend and alumnus of Wesleyan will want to own this volume. The historical data which it records will be of interest to everyone. Yet beyond this is the concern of the church which brought the college into being and the concern of the church which has reached a new high in its support of the college. Professor Plummer has given a reliable picture of this relationship. As further justification of his point of view it may be noted that his financial statement ended with the year 1963-64. Since he wrote the book, we have had another year's accounting showing an increase in support by the West Virginia Conference of over $40,000 for the year. Methodism's total support of current expenses is now equal to the income of an endowment of four and a half million dollars!

The author has made it clear that the history of a college is in essence the story of the strong men who have been involved in its affairs and the strong men which the college has produced. The latter justify the college: the former make it. One should not be deluded into naming those who have made distinctive contributions to the history of Wesleyan. I shall not succumb. You who have the book in hand will make this discovery for yourself.

The book has made possible to me a perspective of Wesleyan's history which I had not previously had, despite the fact that my acquaintance with it goes back forty years. Doubtless many phases of its history are known in varying degrees by the alumni. Yet this book, designed to be available for the seventy-fifth anniversary of the college, gives the sequence of historical events in such a way as to underscore the dramatic story which brings the college to its present status.

A special word needs to be said about the final chapter of the book. As readers probably know, Wesleyan does not endeavor to excuse its church-relatedness. It boldly states on the cover of its annual catalogue that it is "A Christian College." It is in this final chapter that Professor Plummer deals with the philosophy of such a college. This is an excellent and important treatment of a college's philosophy of education and the implementation of that philosophy in curriculum as well as the relationship of that philosophy to both faculty and student body are really the essence of the college. The chapter makes clear that this is not a static situation. West Virginia Wesleyan constantly examines itself in the light of its philosophy and of contemporary needs.

There is no reason to doubt that Wesleyan's history justifies our confidence in its future.

—FRED G. HOLLOWAY

Bishop
The Methodist Church
West Virginia Area

ACKNOWLEDGMENTS

This account of the history of West Virginia Wesleyan College has been written in observance of the 75th anniversary of Wesleyan to be celebrated during the academic year, 1965-66. It attempts to narrate what I deem to be significant developments in the life of the school from the time when it was only a dream of Methodists in West Virginia to the present. I have recounted the history of Wesleyan with a minimum of editorial comment in the belief that the story of the life and work of the school speaks for itself. Recognizing the limitations of this approach, I present the story with the feeling that it might have been told better by one whose association with Wesleyan has been more intimate and of longer duration than my own.

I am much in debt to the work of Dr. Thomas Haught whose *West Virginia Wesleyan College, 1890-1940* was published on the occasion of the 50th anniversary of the school, and to *West Virginia Wesleyan College, The Sixth Decade, 1940-1950,* which he produced ten years later. The memoirs of Dr. Carl G. Doney, *Cheerful Yesterdays and Confident Tomorrows,* and of Dr. Roy McCuskey, *All Things Work Together for Good to Them that Love God,* have provided much information and insight.

The number of persons who have assisted me in gathering material and in getting various facets of the life of Wesleyan in perspective is legion. However, special thanks is due President Stanley Martin, Dean Orlo Strunk, Jr., *emeriti* professors Dr. Ralph Brown, Dr. Lewis Chrisman, and Dr. James Hupp; and other members of the Wesleyan staff and faculty including Mrs. E. C. Bennett, Mrs. Jean Carden, Mr. Walter Collins, Mr. Raymond Kiser, Mr. James Ling, Mr. Patton Nickell, Mr. James Stansbury, Dr. Walter Brown, Dr. Herbert Coston, Dr. Sidney Davis, Dr. George Glauner, Dr. Dwight Mikkelson, Mr. David Reemsnyder, Miss Helen Stockert, Dr. William Willis and Dr. John Wright.

I am also indebted to Mrs. Eleanor Williams for the loan of her collection of materials from the early years of the school; to Mrs. W. P. Barlow, the Reverend Mr. Arnold Belcher, Mrs. W. C. Thurman, and Mrs. Aquila Ward for assistance in obtaining information about several of the founding fathers; to the Reverend Mr. Lawrence Sherwood for information concerning the Parkersburg Academy. The late Dr. Clyde O. Law

7

performed an invaluable service for me by sharing with me facts and impressions gleaned from his long and productive association with Wesleyan.

Material for the history has been gathered largely from the minutes of the Board of Trustees, the reports and addresses of presidents and deans, the annual bulletins and other publications of the college. Except where indicated, the quotations have come from these materials.

—KENNETH M. PLUMMER

West Virginia Wesleyan College
May 30, 1965

CONTENTS

CONTENTS

I

THE SCHOOL IS LOCATED

Frontiersmen who came into Western Virginia during the late eighteenth and early nineteenth centuries from New England and Eastern Virginia were not lacking in concern for education. This was especially true of the Presbyterians with their deep-rooted interest in learning. However, the initial settlers were harassed by many problems which prevented the development of educational opportunities. In Western Virginia these included a long period of preoccupation with the Indian menace, the time-consuming and physically exhausting task of settling in a wilderness area, the low economic status of the settlers and the nature of the country itself which made for isolation.

From 1800 to the Civil War period the interest of the churches in Western Virginia in education was largely influenced by the revivalism of the Second Great Awakening which flourished on the frontier and resulted in the growth of evangelical Protestant groups. The largest gains were made during this period by the Methodists and the Baptists. The Methodists, with whom we are chiefly concerned, had an ambivalent attitude toward education. They came out of a tradition fostered by the university-trained Wesleys who insisted on the necessity of a union of vital piety and sound learning. The revivals, on the one hand, were an impetus to the desire for learning, in particular the ability to read, since the evangelical revival was centered in the Biblical message. The ability to read the Bible became important to those who wished to search it for its truths. On the other hand, revivalism tended to undercut the growth of education. Ministers in the evangelical tradition believed they were called to preach, and they tended to ignore formal theological training. Indeed, they considered it a detriment to the performance of their function. Moreover, the revivals were used as a means of combatting not only the devil and Calvinists but also Deism. Deism, which came out of the intellectual currents flowing toward America from England and the mainland of Europe, was associated with a tendency to infidelity, the subversion of true religion and sound government. In the fight against

11

Deism or infidelity the revivals engendered a strong suspicion of intellectualism.

The attitude of the frontier Methodist clergy toward education is to be seen in the views of Peter Cartwright who served circuits of the Methodist Church in Western Virginia during the first half of the nineteenth century and was engaged widely in revival activity. He valued study and expressed gratitude to Bishop William McKendree for his small attainments in literature and divinity. Nevertheless, he scoffed at the Presbyterians and other branches of the Protestant church who contended for an educated ministry. The illiterate Methodist preachers, he affirmed, actually set the world on fire while they were lighting their matches. He feared that an educated Methodist clergy would make inroads on the itinerant ministry by localizing, secularizing and softening it.

> I awfully fear for our beloved Methodism. Multiply colleges, universities, seminaries and academies, multiply our agencies and editorships, and fill them all with our best and most efficient preachers, and you localize and secularize them too; then farewell to the itinerancy . . . and when that takes place farewell to Methodism.[1]

Cartwright represents the typical attitude toward a "called" rather than an educated ministry. In 1856, writing of his early years in the ministry, he recalls:

> A Methodist preacher in those days, when he felt that God had called him to preach, instead of hunting up a college or Biblical Institute, hunted up a hardy pony of a horse, and some traveling apparatus, and with his library always at hand, namely, Bible, Hymn-Book and Discipline, he started with a text that never wore out nor grew stale, he cried, "Behold the Lamb of God, that taketh away the sins of the world." [2]

The use of Bible, Hymn-Book and Discipline would require at least a minimal education. Beyond this, the frontier Methodist clergy were suspicious of higher education, at least for the clergy, and reflect an anti-intellectualism typical of the time and still engrained in the American culture.

The success of the revival movement in bringing large numbers of persons into the church, along with other factors, gradually changed the configuration of the church and its attitude toward education. At the beginning of the nineteenth century even meeting houses had been scarce.

---

[1] *Autobiography of Peter Cartwright*, W. P. Strickland, Ed., (Cincinnati: Cranston and Stowe, 1856), p. 81.
[2] *Ibid.*, p. 243.

The itinerant Methodist preacher, penetrating the wilderness, held services in cabins, along the roadside, and sometimes in taverns. The camp meeting, concentrating on the conversion of sinners, was the symbol of frontier religion and revivalism was the typical activity of the churches.

However, the social, cultural and religious climate in America underwent a dramatic change during the nineteenth century, particularly after the Civil War. The country west of the Alleghenies and east of the Mississippi lost its predominantly frontier character. Frontier camp meeting revivalism, with its tendency to undercut the teaching function of the church, gradually waned. Camp meeting sites were turned into meeting places for summer conferences or chatauquas or into middle class summer resorts. The growth of towns and cities and of more adequate church buildings called for a settled clergy. The Wesleyan heritage emerged again and an educated leadership gradually came to the fore in the Methodist Church. The educational and cultural gap between the clergy of the Methodist Church and the clergy of the Presbyterian, Congregational and Episcopal Churches slowly closed. The changed attitude toward education was given impetus by the growing influence of the religious education movement with its roots in the views of Horace Bushnell and its emphasis upon Christian nurture rather than radical conversion.

The change in the Methodist attitude toward education began before the Civil War. In 1830 the Methodists had not established a single permanent college. From 1830 to the start of the Civil War they founded thirty-four permanent colleges. In Western Virginia Methodists ventured into the field of education even before they were organized as an annual conference in 1848. The Methodists, along with the Presbyterians and to a lesser extent other denominational groups, established the first academies.[3]

The Methodist Episcopal Church may have controlled the Mount Hebron School at Huntington, West Virginia, prior to 1838, the year it became a chartered institution known as the Marshall Academy under an act passed by the General Assembly of Virginia. The Mount Hebron Church was used as a school prior to this date by several denominations, but there is no evidence that the Methodists had an exclusive interest in the school.[4] The academy came under the control of the Methodist

[3] I am indebted for the discussion of revivalism and its influence to W. W. Sweet, *Revivalism in America* (Charles Scribner's Sons, 1944) and C. C. Cleveland, *The Great Revival in the West*, 1797-1805 (Peter Smith, 1959).

[4] See *West Virginia History*, Vol. 13, No. 2, January, 1952, Robert C. O'Toole, "The Early History of Marshall Academy, 1837-1850."

13

Episcopal Church South in 1850. In 1866 it passed out of control of the church apparently because the church was unable to raise the money to cover the financial liabilities of the school.

On August 3, 1839, the Quarterly Conference of the Little Kanawha Circuit of the Methodist Episcopal Church adopted a memorial petitioning the Ohio Annual Conference to take under its patronage the Parkersburg Male and Female Seminary. The seminary began operation on April 30, 1839, with the Reverend Charles R. Baldwin, the local station preacher, in charge. The memorialists noted "there is no institution of the kind under the patronage of the Methodist Episcopal Church in Western Virginia; nor is it known to your memorialists that there is any academical school now in successful operation in the western part of said state at this time . . . ."[5] The Ohio Conference in its session of 1840 appropriated $100 for the support of the school known as "Asbury Academy." On February 8, 1842, the academy was chartered under Virginia statutes. There is no clear evidence regarding the length of life of the academy. Maxwell P. Gaddis, agent for the seminary, says that during the summer of 1841-42 he raised a subscription of nearly $5,000 for the school. However, the money was never used for the purpose for which it was subscribed. During the following spring difficulties arose which resulted in the abandonment of the project.[6]

In 1842 plans were consummated by the Methodist Episcopal Church for the purchase of the Randolph Academy erected in Clarksburg, West Virginia, in 1795. The Reverend Gordon Batelle, a member of the Pittsburgh Conference, became the principal. The school known as the Northwestern Virginia Academy was operated by the Methodist Church until the Civil War when it was used for military purposes as a prison, soldier's barracks and hospital. Efforts to revive the academy following the war failed. The trustees of the institution reported to the annual conference in 1868 that it was impossible to sustain it as an independent school, and it had been temporarily merged into the free schools of the borough of Clarksburg. The Methodists in 1885 terminated all efforts directed at control or ownership of the academy.

---

[5] This quotation and information regarding the Parkersburg Male and Female Seminary was obtained from the original memorial to the Ohio Annual Conference now owned by the Reverend Dr. Lawrence Sherwood, a member of the West Virginia Annual Conference of The Methodist Church.

[6] Maxwell P. Gaddis, *Footprints of an Itinerant* (Cincinnati: Methodist Book Concern, 1855), pp. 287-89.

The Fairmont Male and Female Seminary, which opened in 1856, came under the patronage and control of the West Virginia Annual Conference of the Methodist Episcopal Church the same year at the request of the trustees of the school. The principal, the Reverend W. R. White, a member of the Baltimore Conference, subsequently became the first State Superintendent of Public Schools in West Virginia. No exact date can be given for the surrender by the Methodists of control of the seminary. There is no reference to the school after 1864 in the minutes of the annual conference.

A step was taken by the church to support the educational program of the conference with the organization in 1851 of the "Educational Society of Western Virginia." The efforts of the society to control the Northwestern Virginia Academy were frustrated by the charter of the institution which prevented any church organization from holding the right of control or private ownership. The support of the society was transferred to the Fairmont Male and Female Seminary. The society, originally incorporated by the State of Virginia, was given recognition by the State of West Virginia, following its establishment, and was re-named "The West Virginia Educational Society." From this point, the society was devoted to providing financial assistance to persons preparing for the ministry.

The failure of the Methodists to sustain the institutions which came under their patronage stems from a number of factors. Chief among them was the lack of adequate financial resources, a problem which also hampered efforts to establish a public school system. The growing strife and sectionalism engendered by the controversy over slavery played a role also. Economic conditions following the Civil War undoubtedly eclipsed attempts to sustain the interest in education.

Following the Civil War it was not until the year 1874, at the session of the West Virginia Annual Conference of the Methodist Episcopal Church in Fairmont, that action was taken looking toward the sponsoring of an educational institution. The Conference Committee on Education stated that reasons too numerous to mention could be advanced for the establishment of one or more conference seminaries. It reported rumors of an offer of buildings, grounds and money ready to be made over to the conference by a gentleman residing in Charleston if it would establish a seminary in the capital of the state. The committee suggested the possibility of reorganizing the academy in Clarksburg or of locating a seminary

15

wherever the most favorable opening should present itself in the northwestern part of the state. A committee was appointed by the annual conference to receive, consider and act on any propositions which might be advanced.

The Committee on Education noted in its report the following year, 1875, that "a generous offer has been made by the citizens of Upshur of subscriptions to the amount of ($3239) thirty-two hundred and thirty-nine dollars and also by the payment of a claim on the United States Government for the use of the Baxter Institute, and in addition a desirable site for a school building is guaranteed if the location of the seminary is made in Buckhannon." The Committee on Conference Seminary, J. G. Blair, J. W. Reger and E. W. Ryan, reported in 1877 that to date the only proposal it had received was from Buckhannon, Upshur County, which had raised its subscription to $6,950 and was offering a site for the seminary containing three acres of land worth at least $1,500, making a total contribution of $8,090. The committee recommended Buckhannon as the location of the seminary and asked that the conference appoint trustees to receive the proposed funds and land, and to proceed with the construction of such buildings as necessary, but not to go beyond the means placed in their hands now or hereafter. Trustees appointed for the seminary at Buckhannon included A. M. Poundstone, G. A. Newlon, E. Leonard, J. W. Heffner, W. R. White, J. W. Reger, and T. B. Hughes.

The records do not make clear what happened to prevent the reception of the Buckhannon proposal. The annual conference adopted a resolution again in 1878 which called for the appointment of a commission of five ministers and four laymen to receive any proposals made by individuals or communities for the location of a seminary provided that none were to be invited from places not accessible, or nearly so, by railroad. The resolution provided further that the school should not be established in any community which could not donate at least $25,000 in lands, buildings or other property; and that the appointment of a majority of the Board of Trustees should be invested in the annual conference. In the light of this action one surmises that the trustees for the seminary at Buckhannon did not believe that the offer which had been made by that community was sufficient. The commission appointed to receive proposals within the limits specified by the resolution included A. C. George, W. R. White, Samuel Steele, E. U. Ryan, and D. H. K. Dix, ministers; H. K.

List, A. I. Boreman, C. M. Bishop, and Nathan Goff, Sr., laymen. The commission met at the Fourth Street Methodist Episcopal Church in Wheeling, February 6, 1879, and elected the Reverend Mr. A. C. George as chairman. The results of this meeting were reported at the fall session of the conference.

> The chairman of the committee was instructed to publish in the church and secular papers an appeal to the friends of education for proposals at some central and accessible point for an academic institution to be founded under the control of the West Virginia Conference of The Methodist Episcopal Church. The appeal was printed in the daily papers of Wheeling, in weekly papers generally throughout the State and The New York Advocate, Pittsburgh Advocate, and Cincinnati Advocate. The purpose of the Seminary was stated in the following terms: "It is intended that this seminary shall be for both sexes and shall provide a higher order of instruction than that of the public schools and such as is necessary to prepare students for admission to the college or university or to fit them for the practical duties of business life and the just demands of society. While the seminary will be under denominational supervision, it will not be a sectarian institution in any proper sense. It is deemed necessary for the success of such an institution, its efficiency and prosperity, that some church organization shall be responsible for its character and work. Manners and morals will be taught as well as science and literature, and the duty of loving and serving God and of accepting Jesus Christ as the Savior of the soul will be diligently inculcated. In a word it is hoped to establish a Christian seminary which shall be not only a help to learning but also a fountain of piety.

The appeal further noted the required $25,000 minimum as well as the need for equipment, library, and other items, plus the necessity of partial endowment for the seminary, with an endowment of not less than $100,000 a foreseeable necessity. On the basis of these terms and conditions, the appeal asked for proposals from different communities for the establishment of the seminary in their localities.

Subsequent meetings of the committee were held in Grafton and Parkersburg. As a result of these meetings it was ascertained that there was general recognition that the proposed seminary would be a boon to any community. But leading citizens in various communities had suggested that if the community in which the seminary were to be located was going to be required to furnish $25,000 in money and other assets, the annual conference should agree to raise an equal amount towards the endowment of the seminary. The committee felt that this was a reasonable suggestion, and that "the West Virginia Conference with 150 traveling preachers, 376 churches, over 33,000 members, and a church property which is in the aggregate put down at $622,120" could and ought to raise money for the endowment of the seminary. The annual conference approved the report provided no measures be taken by which the conference would become financially involved.

The following year, 1880, the annual conference Committee on Education recommended the appointment of "a committee of ten to solicit subscriptions for an Institution of Academic Grade for both sexes to be located south of the Little Kanawha River," and a Board of Control to purchase or erect a building, should it be deemed necessary, and to commence and control a school until the next session of the annual conference. The board could not act, however, unless the full amount of $25,000 were raised. Sectional interests may have prompted this move to establish the school in the southern part of the state.

In 1883 the annual conference appointed a Committee on Centennial Celebration of the Anniversary of Methodism in America. The report of the committee included the following recommendation:

> That the erection and endowment of an institution of learning of high grade for both sexes be one of the principal objects of the thank-offerings of our people of this Conference. The location of said institution to be fixed by the Conference at a future session.

The Committee for the Celebration of the Centennial recommended in 1884 that each charge should take an offering and solicit funds publicly and privately to be equally divided between the permanent fund for worn out preachers and the widows and orphans of deceased ministers and the building and endowment of a conference seminary. As of September 9, 1886, the Centennial Fund had raised a total of $283.57 for the proposed seminary.

In 1886 the Committee on Education suggested that the strategy of "waiting for something to turn up" had failed hopelessly. Let the Board of Trustees secure a charter of incorporation and locate the seminary as speedily as possible! Let the second Sunday of January be observed to present the interest of the proposed school to the churches and let collections and subscriptions be taken! Let the money in the hands of the treasurer of the educational fund and the funds held by the Board of Control of the Centennial Education Fund be handed over to the Board of Trustees of the seminary as soon as it be incorporated and organized!

The Reverend Mr. John W. Reger who had been appointed a trustee for the seminary had voiced his sentiments regarding the proposed school in a letter published in *The Pittsburgh Christian Advocate*, March 3, 1887. He noted that among the imperative reasons for founding an institution of high school grade in West Virginia was the fact that each year the state lost some of its most promising young men, and that many preachers transferred to other conferences because of the inability to secure an education for themselves or their families within the state. The paramount question facing 40,000 Methodists in West Virginia was whether or not they would act to afford educational opportunities within their own state in a location that would provide educational advantages for the greatest number. Inasmuch as the northern tier of counties in the state had educational advantages near at hand in old and well established institutions under the control and patronage of the church, it would be a mistake to try to establish a school there. The Reverend Mr. Reger felt that the conference had made a grave mistake when it adopted such action as was calculated to lead people to believe that the seminary would be located at the place giving the largest amount of money or property inducement. Unless the men appointed to locate the seminary could rise above local influences and local prejudices, and discard bargain and sale, there was great danger that they would make a sad and irreparable mistake. The seminary, he maintained, would be most accessible and provide the greatest educational advantage if it were located in the interior of the state.

Interest in a Methodist controlled school during this period was doubtless influenced by other factors than the exodus of students from the state or the lack of educational opportunities within the state. Charles A. Ambler in *A History of Education in West Virginia* notes the fact that following the formation of the State of West Virginia prominent Methodists manned most of the important positions in the new state government. Methodists came to regard the State University at Morgantown as their school and urged their constituents to patronize it and the state normal schools. The interest of the Methodists in establishing an institution of their own waxed and waned depending upon whether or not the university had a Methodist president. In 1882 the Methodists lost control of the university. The university adopted the curriculum of the University of Virginia. These events produced an exodus of Methodist students from the university.

Impetus to the establishment of a school where boys and girls could

19

be educated under Christian influence may have come also from the growing recognition that the theory of evolution was being taught at many universities.

In its annual plea for the establishment of a seminary, the annual conference Committee on Education in 1887 affirmed:

> Loyalty to Methodism as well as to the Church Catholic compels us to turn our patronage into those channels only which promise to bring the young into the communion of Saints. No college that permits its professors to insinuate skepticism into immature and impressible minds, who antagonize scripture with science falsely so-called can expect any favor from Christian parents. It is demanded that every man should be presented perfect in Jesus Christ as well as perfect in the curriculum of study.

This was the period when the rumblings of controversy were being heard in the churches over the attempt to reconcile the Bible with the findings of science, in particular, the theory of emergent evolution which undercut the Biblical story of creation. In addition, the work of Biblical scholars in Europe who were applying the historical-critical method to the study of the scriptures was beginning to make itself felt in the theological schools in America. In his autobiography, *All Things Work Together for Good to Them That Love God,* Dr. Roy McCuskey notes that around the turn of the century the West Virginia Annual Conference of the Methodist Episcopal Church did not have a large number of seminary graduates.[7] The atmosphere was conservative and much was heard about "higher criticism" and "evolution." Dr. McCuskey and several of his friends who decided to attend the Boston School of Theology were stoutly opposed and discouraged by several of the older ministers. The focal point of opposition was Professor Hinckley G. Mitchell who was a storm center of controversy at Boston for about fifteen years because of his introduction of higher criticism in the study of the Bible.

Members of the Methodist Episcopal Church were also aware of the fact that even while they were talking about establishing a school, the Methodist Episcopal Church South was considering a proposition to establish an institution at Philippi, West Virginia. The seminary at Philippi did not materialize. However, in 1888 the southern branch of the church opened a seminary at Barboursville in Cabell County.

The Board of Trustees appointed for the seminary met at the Methodist Episcopal Church in Buckhannon on April 13, 1887. Present were the

---

[7] Roy McCuskey, *All Things Work Together for Good to Them That Love God* (Buckhannon, W. Va.: West Virginia Wesleyan Press, 1964).

Reverends A. J. Lyda, L. K. Jordan, J. A. Fullerton, J. W. Reger, E. H. Orwin, L. L. Stewart, A. B. Rohrbough, the Honorable H. C. McWhorter, Captain A. M. Poundstone, and John A. Bonner, Esquire. A. J. Lyda was elected chairman. Propositions for location of the seminary were received from Grafton, Kingwood, Philippi, Salem, Weston, Wheeling, Clarksburg, and Buckhannon. Two more meetings were held before a decision was reached, with additional propositions coming from Parkersburg, Wirt Court House and Elizabeth. On July 13, at Philippi, thirteen of the sixteen members of the Board of Trustees chose Buckhannon as the site for the school on the thirteenth ballot. The sixteen members of the Board of Trustees were divided evenly between ministers and laymen. All were currently citizens of West Virginia.

The Reverend Dr. John Archer Fullerton (1850-1928) was a native of Belfast, Ireland. He entered the ministry at twenty years of age and preached at Glen Arm and Carnlough near Belfast. He became a member of the West Virginia Annual Conference of the Methodist Episcopal Church in 1872. In addition to pastorates, he served one term as a district superintendent. For a time he was editor of the *Methodist Episcopal Times,* published at Parkersburg.

The Reverend Dr. Andrew Jackson Lyda (1821-1900) was a native of Hancock, Maryland. Before the seminary was established he was the first chairman of the Board of Trustees. Upon location of the seminary he resigned as chairman to become the financial agent for the school. Mr. Lyda was a charter member of the West Virginia Annual Conference and spent forty-four of his forty-eight years in the effective ministry in West Virginia. He was chaplain of the Third Virginia Volunteers, the United States Army, from 1862-1864.

The Reverend Mr. E. H. Orwen (1835-1892) was a native of Delhi, New York. After a brief career as a teacher, he entered the ministry and from 1852 served churches in New York and West Virginia. On two occasions during his ministry he was forced by ill health to take the supernumerary relation. He engaged in editorial work during one of these periods. At the time of the founding of the seminary he was engaged in assisting his son in establishing a newspaper at Aberdeen, Maryland. He was secretary of the Board of Trustees until his death. He was also a trustee of Ohio Wesleyan University.

The Reverend Dr. John W. Reger (1815-1893) was born near Volga, West Virginia. At the age of twenty-two he was licensed to preach by the

21

Methodist Episcopal Church at a quarterly meeting held near French Creek. He was sent as junior preacher to the Randolph Circuit which covered a territory of three hundred miles from the Mingo Flats on the headwaters of the Tygart River to Allegany County, Maryland. He served for forty-seven years in the Pittsburgh and West Virginia Conferences. In 1861 he enlisted as a private in the 7th West Virginia Volunteer Infantry and served until after the battle of Gettysburg. He was forced to resign because of illness, but he served as chaplain at the Grafton Hospital until the close of the War between the States. He gave ardent support to the location of the seminary at Buckhannon where he lived during his retirement. The laborers who erected the original seminary building said that he spent the greater part of his time on the grounds during the construction examining every brick and stone that went into the structure. A few days before his death he informed a friend that he considered his contribution to the location and building of the West Virginia Conference Seminary the crowning act of his life.

The Reverend Mr. A. B. Rohrbough (1836-1901) was born near Buckhannon, West Virginia. He was admitted on trial to the West Virginia Annual Conference in 1857. During 1862-63 he lived in Illinois where he taught school. For the next ten years he was a resident of Buckhannon and engaged in newspaper work, teaching and temperance work. During two of these years he was superintendent of the public schools. He returned to the Southern Illinois Conference for another ten-year period during which he served as a pastor. In 1884 he returned to West Virginia as a pastor, and for a period of two years he again engaged in newspaper and temperance work at Buckhannon. In 1900 he was appointed editor of the *Methodist Episcopal Times*.

The Reverend Mr. Loren L. Stewart (1845-1893) came to West Virginia from Allegheny County, Pennsylvania. He was admitted on trial to the West Virginia Annual Conference in 1870 and served as a pastor and as presiding elder for two terms.

The Reverend Mr. William R. White (1820-1893) was born in Georgetown, District of Columbia. Mr. White, a graduate of Dickinson College, served as pastor of churches in the Baltimore Conference of the Methodist Episcopal Church from 1844 to 1852. He became president of Olin and Preston Institute, Blacksburg, Virginia, in 1852. From 1856 to 1863 he was president of the Male and Female Seminary, Fairmont, West Virginia. Mr. White was the first state superintendent of the free school system of West Virginia from 1864-69. During 1869-70 he was president of the state normal school at Fairmont. He returned to the pastorate for a period of twelve years during which he served as presiding elder of the Buckhannon District from 1879-83. The year before his death he was principal of the Buckhannon graded schools, and during 1892-93 he was principal of the Fairmont graded schools.

John C. Bardall (1839-1925) was born at sea while his parents were emigrating to America from Germany. At the age of nineteen he began to learn the trade of whip manufacturer at Wellsburg, Pennsylvania. He worked for several whip manufacturers successively until 1873 when he helped establish the firm of Weaver and Bardall at the Western Penitentiary of Pennsylvania. In 1877 the firm located at Moundsville, West Virginia. The firm also operated a tannery in Pittsburgh for its supply of leather. Mr. Bardall had interests in the natural gas, coal and fire clay lands around Moundsville and Wheeling. He served for over a decade as superintendent of the Sunday School of the Methodist Episcopal Church at Moundsville. He was a lay delegate to the General Conference of the Methodist Episcopal Church at New York City in 1888, and a reserve delegate to the Ecumenical Council of all Protestant churches which met in New York in 1890. He was a member of the building committee of the Simpson Methodist Church, Moundsville, in 1907, and a member of the Board of Trustees of the church until about 1915. He also helped to establish the Calvary and Glendale Methodist Churches.

Mr. John A. Barnes (1854-1936) was a native of Lewis County, West Virginia. Mr. Barnes was a merchant in Weston. He helped organize the Citizens Bank of Weston and was an official of the bank until 1934. He was one of the organizers of the Building and Loan Association and a member of the Board of Directors from 1887-1936. An active layman in the First Methodist Church of Weston, he was a member of the Official Board and of the Board of Trustees; choir director, 1875-1916; a Sunday school teacher, 1925-36; and Boy Scoutmaster, 1912-14. During World War I he was director of the Weston Red Cross. Mr. Barnes was one of fifty men to buy the first plot of acreage at Jackson's Mill for the original 4-H Camp. He served as secretary of the Board of Trustees of Wesleyan.

The Honorable Benjamin F. Martin (1828-1895) was born at Farmington, West Virginia. He graduated from Allegheny College in 1854, studied law and was admitted to the bar in 1856. He settled in Pruntytown, West Virginia, but moved to Grafton when that town was made the county seat. He entered politics and was elected to the United States Congress in 1876 on the Democratic ticket. He was an active layman in the Methodist Episcopal Church.

Samuel Phillips McCormick (1841-1889), a native of Washington County, Pennsylvania, attended the Fairmont Academy. He worked for two years as a brick mason before teaching school in Marion and Monongalia counties in West Virginia from 1858 to the outbreak of the Civil War. Beginning July 1861, he served for approximately a year in General Bank's Division of the Army of the Potomac. He was honorably discharged because of a chronic illness. After studying law under the direction of Judge Ralph L. B. Berkshire at Morgantown, he located at Harrisville, Ritchie County. He moved to West Union in 1865, and the following year he was elected prosecuting attorney. He located at Grafton in 1873, and beginning in 1876 served a four-year term as prosecuting attorney of Taylor County. In 1880 he was elected as a delegate-at-large from West Virginia to the Republican National Convention, and was one of three delegates who created a national sensation by refusing to vote for Senator Roscoe Conkling's resolution binding delegates in advance of a nomination to support the party candidates. He served for eight years as a member of the Republican State Executive Committee. In 1885 he was appointed collector of internal revenue for West Virginia by President Chester Arthur.

The Honorable Henry C. McWhorter (1836-1913) was born in Marion County, Ohio. At the outbreak of the Civil War he served in the home guards for several months. In September 1861, he enlisted as a private in the Federal Army and rose to the rank of captain. Forced to retire in 1862, he served to the end of the war as chief clerk in the Provost Marshall's office. Meanwhile, he studied law with his brother, Judge Marcellus McWhorter. He was admitted to the bar in West Virginia in 1866 and began the practice of law in Charleston. He was active in the Republican Party and was elected to the state legislature 1865-68, 1885-87. He was speaker of the House of Delegates in 1868. He served at various times as prosecuting attorney of Kanawha County, and as postmaster and city solicitor of Charleston. In 1896 he was elected to the Supreme Court of Appeals of West Virginia and served as presiding judge from 1906 to 1909. Mr. McWhorter was a member of the Charleston Methodist Church in which he served as Sunday school superintendent and as a member of the Board of Trustees. He was a Universalist in his religious beliefs, and he described himself as a "Universal Methodist." He was president of the Board of Trustees of Wesleyan from 1897 until his death.

Mr. A. M. Poundstone (1835-1921) was a native of Fayette County, Pennsylvania. After graduation from Allegheny College, he taught school at New Lexington, Ohio. He began the study of law and was admitted to the bar in 1860. He served in the Federal Army with the rank of captain until his discharge in 1865. He immediately came to Buckhannon, West Virginia, and opened a law office. In 1886 he was elected prosecuting attorney for Upshur County and served in this office for fourteen years. He was a member for two terms, 1872-79, in the West Virginia State Legislature. He was an active member of the First Methodist Episcopal Church in Buckhannon.

Mr. William A. Wilson (1842-1920) was a native of Wheeling, West Virginia, where he was a lumber dealer, planing mill operator and building contractor. He took over his father's concern, under the name of W. A. Wilson and Sons, and operated a wholesale and retail business covering five states. For a number of years he was president of the Commercial Bank of Wheeling. Mr. Wilson was a member of the North Street Methodist Episcopal Church in Wheeling.

Samuel Woods (1822-1897) was born in East Canada. His family moved to Meadville, Pennsylvania, when he was a boy. He graduated from Allegheny College in 1842, then studied law in Pittsburgh. He taught for a time at Morgantown and settled in 1848 in Barbour County or the Philippi District where he practiced law. He was a member of the convention at Richmond, Virginia, in 1861, which adopted an ordinance of secession from the Union. He espoused the cause of the Confederacy and served in the Confederate Army. His family refugeed south and returned to Philippi with the cessation of hostilities. In 1872 Mr. Woods was a member of the Second Constitutional Convention which prepared the constitution for the State of West Virginia. He served as a judge of the West Virginia Supreme Court of Appeals from 1883-88. He served as chairman of the Board of Trustees of the West Virginia Conference Seminary from the founding of the school until his death.

Information regarding one of the original trustees is scanty. The Reverend Mr. L. H. Jordan was a member of the West Virginia Annual Conference of the Methodist Episcopal Church until around the turn of the century when his name was no longer listed in the annual conference journal. The recollection of several persons in Buckhannon is that he served a term as district superintendent of the Buckhannon District. During his travels on the district he gathered many seedling oak trees which he planted on the seminary campus.

On July 16, the board, after considering various sites, took an option on "60 acres, more or less" offered by William F. Carper at $80 per acre and authorized use of as much of "money subscribed by citizens of Upshur County and others" as "may be necessary to pay and satisfy the price agreed to be given for the Carper option." On August 29, the board rescinded this action because it appeared that the trustees would have to assume the burden of building a bridge across the Buckhannon River to the Carper property in North Buckhannon, and because the property contained deep ravines. It accepted instead a proposition from Levi Leonard of "43 acres, 1 rod and 13 square poles of land" for the price of $5,551.86. The trustees made a down payment of $300 and arranged for the residue to be paid "in three equal installments of $1,750.62 each with interest from date, payable and lien to be reserved on the land conveyed to secure the deferred payments." The Reverend Dr. J. W. Reger assumed personal responsibility for the down payment to be reimbursed out of collections on subscriptions to the seminary. P. C. Lewis of Buckhannon was employed at a fee of two dollars to plant four square stones, one at each of the four corners of the purchased land. At long last the seminary was on the way.

The location and subsequent establishment of the seminary at Buckhannon brought to fruition a long standing interest in education among the residents of Upshur County.

The General Assembly of Virginia on February 1, 1847, passed an act entitled "An Act to incorporate the male and female academy of Buckhannon" on petition of several citizens in and around the town. The incorporators purchased a lot on West Main Street about a block west of the present intersection of Main and Locust Streets and erected a two-story schoolhouse. The school was abandoned after several years and the building deteriorated. In 1866 the West Virginia Legislature appointed trustees for the property. The trustees sold the property and put the money on interest until such time as another high school should be established.

Subsequent impetus for the founding of a school in Upshur County

26

came when the Presbyterians attempted to establish a high school at Buckhannon. The pastor, the Reverend Mr. R. Lawson, persuaded his parishioners to name the school after Richard Baxter, an English Protestant educator. The site selected, now part of the Wesleyan campus, was known as the Oak Grove and stretched from the intersection of the present Sedgwick Street and College Avenue to the Annie Merner Pfeiffer Library. The contract for the building was let and lumber was hauled to the site. Before the building was erected, McClellan's troops invaded Upshur County and appropriated the lumber for camps and camp fires. In 1905 the United States awarded the Presbyterian Church in Buckhannon $1,431 damages for destruction of property. As we have previously noted, the first overture made from Upshur County for the location of the seminary at Buckhannon included the offer of the resources of the Baxter Institute.

Again in 1871 the Presbyterians, immigrants from New England who settled in and around French Creek, secured a charter for the French Creek Institute. The school, a male and female academy designed to train teachers and promote education generally, functioned for about fourteen years.

The West Virginia Normal and Classical Academy was incorporated and located in Buckhannon in 1882, with the United Brethren in Christ's Church as the founders and promoters. The academy, housed in a ten-room frame building, was a male and female seminary. The curriculum, following the typical pattern of the times, included five courses—classical, philosophical, musical, commercial, and teacher training. The academy aimed at preparing students for entrance in the sophomore year of college and at qualifying students for teaching in the public schools of the state. Professor W. O. Mills, a graduate of Oberlin University, took charge of the school in 1889. When the school moved to Mason City, West Virginia, in 1897, Mr. Mills became professor of mathematics at the West Virginia Conference Seminary. The corporation of Buckhannon purchased the property and converted it into a public school, the present Academy Elementary School.

These abortive attempts to establish a school do not appear to have slackened the interest of the residents of Upshur County in education.

The Board of Trustees reported the location of the seminary in Buckhannon to the annual conference meeting in Parkersburg, October 5, 1887, and noted that it had received from the citizens of Buckhannon

27

and Upshur County good and solvent subscriptions to the sum of $12,000, payable one-fourth when work on the buildings should be commenced, the balance in three equal payments at three, six and nine months thereafter. The Reverend Mr. A. J. Lyda was appointed as financial agent for the seminary, whereupon he resigned as president of the board. The trustees, meeting during the session, elected Samuel Woods president, an office which he filled until his death in 1897. B. F. Martin, L. H. Jordan and W. R. White were appointed a committee to secure the services of a competent architect to furnish plans and specifications for a building not to exceed in cost $25,000. A. M. Poundstone was authorized to employ workmen to quarry and deliver upon the seminary ground building rock subscribed by Mr. M. Jackson. The board also presented papers of incorporation for approval by the annual conference which called for sixteen trustees, eight ministers and eight laymen, to be elected annually from the membership of the Methodist Episcopal Church living within the bounds of the West Virginia Annual Conference. It further requested the annual conference to apportion $1,500 to the churches to meet expenses of the seminary agent and to fix the first Sunday in December as Seminary Day for collections to meet the apportionment.

The board met again in Buckhannon, April 11-13, 1888. A committee consisting of J. C. Bardall, S. P. McCormick, A. M. Poundstone, H. C. McWhorter, L. H. Jordan, and J. W. Reger, was appointed to receive bids for the erection of a seminary building and to enter contract for it according to the plans and specifications prepared by Mr. E. Wells, architect, of Wheeling. The trustees visited the seminary grounds in a body and decided to locate the building 350 feet from the front of the parcel of land and 300 feet from the proposed street to the southwest. They subsequently rescinded this plan and declared that the northerly side of the building should parallel Seminary Avenue (now College Avenue) to place it on the crest of the knoll. The trustees also appointed L. H. Jordan, J. W. Reger and A. M. Poundstone of Buckhannon as an executive committee to pass on bills for the treasurer, B. F. Martin, of Grafton.

By August 30, 1888, A. J. Lyda was able to report cash and subscriptions of $1,905.05, in addition to the collection of $260 prior to his appointment as agent. The board awarded a contract for excavation and stone work to George Crabb on a bid of $4,167 less $175 per perch on all stone furnished by the trustees, the work to be completed by May

15, 1889. Meeting again on October 10 and 11, the board authorized its president to enter into contract with Henry O'Blenness for erection and completion of the superstructure of the seminary building at the price of $23,332, to be enclosed by December 1889, and to be completed before the first day of July, 1890. Permission was given to make bricks from clay to be dug from the campus.

In view of the fact that the treasurer's report showed a balance on hand of only $1,689.76, the board adopted a resolution presented by Samuel Woods authorizing the raising of $15,000 through the sale of ". . . one hundred fifty coupon bonds of one hundred dollars each issued by this board payable ten years from and after the first of January, 1889, with interest thereon at the rate of six per cent annual, payable annually at the Buckhannon Bank in the town of Buckhannon, West Virginia. . . ." The bonds were secured by a deed of trust on the forty-three acres of land. In addition, twelve of the trustees signed a note for $3,000 borrowed from the First National Bank of Grafton. The board authorized the treasurer to collect subscriptions as they became due and urged the securing of new pledges.

The following spring L. H. Jordan and A. M. Poundstone, who had been appointed to explore the possibility of opening the seminary in September 1889, before completion of the building, reported a possible enrollment of fifty students for the fall and winter terms and one hundred for the spring and summer terms. They based their estimate on the response to a circular sent to the ministers of the annual conference, few of whom responded. In view of the pressure which would be on the trustees to get the building up, they did not believe it was possible to plan for an early opening. A year later at their annual meeting, June 11-13, 1890, at Buckhannon, the trustees set an autumn opening date of September 10, and voted to tender to the Reverend Mr. Bennett W. Hutchinson the presidency of the seminary at a salary of $1,200, and to his wife the work of the music department with the profits thereof as compensation. The board rounded out its preparation by fixing tuition for the first year at $25, ministers' children at one-half tuition; by appointing a committee to arrange a prospectus for the fall term and advertise in such newspapers "as will gratuitously do so," and the *Pittsburgh Conference Advocate;* and by hiring Professor Jay F. Ogden to organize and administer a teacher training program, and Miss Emma Tavenner to teach history and English. By the opening of school it had hired Mr. Frank Trotter to teach Latin, German and French and D. T. E. Castelle, M.D., to teach chemistry, physiology and zoology.

Bennett W. Hutchinson came to the presidency of the seminary at the age of thirty-one. He received the A. B. Degree at Ohio Wesleyan University in 1883, and taught for a year at Augusta College, Augusta, Kentucky. After serving another year as a circuit riding preacher at Sistersville, West Virginia, he entered the Boston University School of Theology and graduated in 1887 with the S.T.B. Degree. He was ordained a Methodist minister and served as pastor of the Emmanuel Church at Mansfield, Massachusetts, and the St. Paul's Methodist Church, Providence, Rhode Island. In 1890, while pastor at St. Paul's, he made the following entry in his diary:

> June 13—Last night received a telegram announcing my election as President of the West Virginia Conference Seminary, Buckhannon, West Virginia and think probably I will accept it. It is a hard but important field.

He accepted the offer and arrived in Buckhannon in July to prepare for the commencement of school on September 3, 1890. His decision to come to the seminary fulfilled a desire to get into the field of education which had persisted from his days at Ohio Wesleyan and had grown with the years. An entry in his diary for October 12, 1884, notes:

> Before I left West Virginia, I almost felt sometimes as though I would like to remain in the Conference and help to work up a Conference school. There is certainly a great work to do in that line in West Virginia. Brother Wilding urged me to remain with that end in view.

One month before receiving the call to the presidency of the seminary he noted that the old inclination toward educational work was as strong as ever.

President Hutchinson later recalled that when he first set foot on the campus no streets were opened except one leading to a gate at the southwest corner of the grounds. The three-story seminary building stood on the site of the present Administration Building. It was a brick structure of good architectural design containing a large and a small chapel, nine recitation rooms, two literary society halls, and the president's office. It was ample for the first years of school, but the building looked lonesome standing alone in a field with no walks or other improvements and no furnishings of any kind. The paraphernalia of the construction crew still littered the grounds, and the pits from which clay had been dug to make bricks scarred the landscape. More than half of the cost of the property was covered by a mortgage bond issue and there was no money in the treasury. The trustees had spent approximately $38,500 for the seminary grounds and building, and when the school opened for classes on September 3, 1890, there was a total debt remaining of $20,000 at six per cent annual interest.

President Hutchinson, with the assistance of Professor Ogden, prepared and distributed a four-page prospectus which listed the names of the faculty and the positions yet to be filled, the location and facilities of the school and the design, scope and religious orientation of the school. While the charter of the school gave it full college powers, during the first year and for several subsequent years, the curriculum was devoted to secondary work only.

In regard to the location and building the prospectus noted:

> The Seminary starts off with a most encouraging outlook. Buckhannon is almost an ideal location, a beautiful country town, near the centre of the State, free from saloons, well supplied with churches, and probably as free from evil influences as any town of the size in the State. The people are hospitable and intelligent, and are ready to extend a cordial welcome to our students.
> The splendid new Seminary building is the best school or college building in the state; beautiful, substantial, convenient, and admirably adapted to school purposes. It is of brick, 106 x 80 feet, three stories in height, and stands upon an eminence overlooking the river and town. It is only a few minutes walk from the centre of town and railroad station. The institution is to be congratulated on the acquirement of such a valuable property. Students coming via Grafton or Parkersburg will leave the B & O R.R. at Clarksburg and reach Buckhannon by the West Virginia and Pittsburgh R.R. Two trains daily.

There was no money for furnishings and equipment, but enough of these were acquired by various means to make possible the opening of school. The Reverend Dr. John W. Reger advanced the money to buy chairs for the chapel and classrooms. A gift of school desks came from the defunct Wheeling College. Donations and a few purchases provided furnishings for the president's office, window shades, a second-hand piano and a carpet for the chapel platform. Since there were no residence halls, the seventy students who enrolled for the first term of ten weeks were housed in carefully selected homes in Buckhannon.

In response to the invitation extended by the Board of Trustees, the annual conference in session at Weston attended in a body the dedication service held October 4, 1890, in the auditorium of the seminary. The *Buckhannon Delta* for October 8, 1890, reported the event.

> The Methodist Episcopal Conference, which was in session at Weston, came to Buckhannon in a body last Saturday for the purpose of dedicating the Seminary at this place. Coming by special train they arrived about ten o'clock and reported immediately to the Seminary Building where interesting services were held. Several addresses were made on the subject of education, Bishop Foss and Rev. W. R. White being among the speakers. Contributions amounting to about $2,500 were received for the Seminary. The members of the conference were entertained by the citizens of Buckhannon for dinner.
>
> A large number of people were in attendance from the town and surrounding country besides those who came on the special train from Weston. In all, there were probably twenty-five hundred people in attendance. The large chapel was full and many could not be accommodated. The building is a grand structure and is justly the pride of our people.

II

FROM SEMINARY TO COLLEGE

The first student to enroll in the seminary on opening day was Mr. Roy Reger of Buckhannon, West Virginia. Seventy students were enrolled for the first term of ten weeks. The total enrollment for the year was two hundred and one. One hundred sixty-seven students were enrolled in the Classical, Literary, Scientific and Normal Courses. The balance were in the Department of Art, Music and Business.

The Literary Department consisted of four courses: the Classical Course, the Scientific Course, the Literary or modern Language Course, and the Normal School. The Literary Course set the pattern for all three courses. Each required work in ancient or modern languages, mathematics, history, natural science, Bible and English. All courses allowed the student to elect some studies suited to his individual taste or adapted to his prospective calling in life.

The Music Department offered a four-year course in piano and instruction in organ and voice. Some students combined music with work in literary studies or art. The Art Department aimed to develop in the student a correct idea of form, an appreciation of beauty, and the training of the powers of observation.

The Normal School was designed to meet the needs of public school teachers. The school year was divided into three terms. Public school teachers could attend the fall term from September to November, teach school during the winter, and return for the spring term from March to June. Teachers were assigned readings to be completed during the winter, and they were examined on the reading when they returned in the spring.

An act passed by the state legislature of West Virginia in 1895 enabled graduates of the Normal School to obtain second-class state teaching certificates on the same basis as graduates of state schools.

The Business College claimed a degree of thoroughness possessed by no other in the state. Courses in commercial science included business penmanship, correspondence and customs, commercial arithmetic, spelling and law, grammar and bookkeeping. A Stenographic Department offered shorthand, called phonography, and typing. These studies were supplemented with practical experience in running an office. A course in Business Practice furnished the student an amount of money with which he carried on a business with the several offices of the school. Business students were given the opportunity to pursue studies in other departments of the seminary.

During the spring of 1892, Major D. T. E. Castelle of the West Virginia National Guard organized the Military Department, also referred to as the Department of Physical Culture. Physical activity consisted of regular army drill. Students wore a uniform of cadet gray including trousers, coat and cap. This program was replaced in 1893-94 by a Department of Physical Culture based on the Delsarte system of calisthenics.

All students were required to participate in such exercises as declamation, essays and in the study of the English classics. Final examinations were conducted in the presence of a committee of visitors appointed by the West Virginia Annual Conference.

Students who were not prepared academically to do the work offered by the seminary were enrolled in a two-year preparatory course covering a variety of subjects but laying major stress on English and grammar.

No minimum age was set for admission to the seminary, but it was suggested that students under fourteen years of age could not enter to advantage.

Dr. Thomas W. Haught, who enrolled as a student at the seminary for the spring term of that first year, said that due to meager opportunities for secondary education in West Virginia the students in the seminary were somewhat retarded intellectually. The average age of students during the first several years was probably the equivalent of the average age of college students today. This fact made the problem of discipline fairly easy, since many of the students already had borne serious responsibilities and were in earnest about getting an education.

President Hutchinson's appraisal of the results of the first year in the life of the seminary was optimistic.

> The record of the first year of the institution has been a pleasant surprise to many of the most sanguinary friends of the enterprise. The Seminary has, in a very short time, taken front rank both in attendance and in the character of its work as well as in the advantages afforded. It is no longer a question whether the time has come to establish the school; the record of the first year has answered that question. The success of the institution is without parallel in the history of the state.

34

The school began the year, said President Hutchinson, with "no alumni, no old students, no precedents, no catalogue, no courses of study, no regulations, no money, but with large faith in the ultimate outcome." During the year the course of study had been established, and the small teaching force had been strengthened by the addition of persons in the music and art departments and in the Normal School. A small amount of apparatus and chemicals had been purchased for the Scientific Course. Several partly paid-for articles of furniture—two pianos, one organ, tables—had been placed in the building. A number of collections of books had been given to the library, and eight hundred other books. About fifty dollars in cash, after expenses, had been donated to the school as the result of a "Book Reception" call in May. Gifts had come to the school during the year which included a pulpit Bible, twenty-five dollars for a carpet for the chapel, a microscope and other items.

In view of the limited facilities and resources available, however, it had been impossible to achieve the ideal of what the school ought to be.

> We have been hedged in and cramped in our work by lack of funds so necessary to build up a great institution of learning. We have *begun* the struggle through which so many schools and colleges of the Church have passed, or are now passing. How long this struggle is to continue no one can tell, but it will be until large and generous gifts are poured into our treasury which shall relieve us of all debt and insure a permanent income from endowment.

The first year had made it clear that there would be no lack of students; the struggle the school faced was a financial one. Giving to education, President Hutchinson told the trustees, was something new in West Virginia, especially among the Methodists. It would require years of work to bring people up to the desired standard of giving.

In his first annual report to the Board of Trustees, the president affirmed that the greatest need of the school, aside from relief from the crushing indebtedness, was a ladies' dormitory and boarding hall. Such a facility would bring to the school many young ladies who would not come otherwise. Also, the clear profit from the dormitory eventually would help to pay deficits in current expenses. This possibility loomed large in his thinking since there was little hope of paying the running expenses of the school with tuition fees alone, especially at the low rates the institution was compelled to charge. President Hutchinson advised the erection of a three-story brick building containing parlors, dining room, kitchen, laundry, rooms for several professors, and music rooms at an estimated cost of $25,000.

President Hutchinson was authorized to advertise the need for the ladies' hall. At the spring meeting of the Board of Trustees in 1892, a committee of five including President Hutchinson, B. F. Martin, J. S. Withers, L. H. Jordan and C. B. Graham was appointed to proceed with plans for the hall. However, the committee was ordered not to build until the indebtedness on the seminary of $20,000 had been provided for and at least $5,000 on pledges for the new building had been obtained. By the fall of 1894, the indebtedness had been covered by cash and pledges, and work had been started on the erection of the dormitory. A gift of $3,000 by the Reverend Mr. John A. Williams added to other resources gave the building committee enough money to meet the restrictions placed upon it by the trustees. However, it was still necessary, in order to proceed with construction, to provide for a bond issue of $18,000 payable ten years after the first day of January, 1895, with interest at 6 per cent payable annually. The building was erected at a cost of about $25,000 according to a rough plan prepared by President Hutchinson and completed by Mr. M. F. Geisy, an architect, of Wheeling, West Virginia. It was ready for occupancy in the autumn of 1895.

The Ladies' Hall had accomodations for sixty students. Overcrowding soon made it necessary to convert an assembly room on the fourth floor into rooms for more students. Living conditions were comfortable, but some facilities were anything but modern, in present-day terms. Dr. Haught notes that a well driven near the outside entrance to the kitchen provided water for the kitchen. Another well located at the end of the walk near Meade Street provided drinking water. Residents of the hall filled pitchers from the well and carried them to their rooms before the beginning of study hours in the evening. A force pump geared to a windmill atop a derrick about fifty feet high pumped water to a tank in the attic of the hall. From the tank the water flowed to the bathrooms, one on each floor. For those occasions when the wind failed to operate the pump, an outside toilet was maintained at the rear of the dormitory. The hall was lighted by electricity, but frequent interruptions in the service made it necessary to keep candles and kerosene lamps at hand. Such emergencies often resulted in the use of these substitutes for more than half the period set apart for study

In the spring of 1892, President Hutchinson, at his own expense, erected a residence on campus near the Oak Grove. The Board of Trustees agreed to purchase the dwelling if his relationship with the college should terminate in any way.

The years of Dr. Hutchinson's presidency were years of financial solvency as far as the current expenses of the school were concerned. Small deficits usually accumulated by the end of each school year, but they were cleared up during the summer months. The year 1895-96 was a typical one. The president reported to the Board of Trustees that receipts for the year were $9,408.88, expenditures were $9,420.29, leaving a deficit of $19.41.

At the spring meeting of the trustees in 1896, it was ascertained that the bond issue of $15,000 dated the first day of January, 1889, had been fully paid, thus relieving the school of the indebtedness incurred in erecting the first building.

In 1892 an extra year of work was added covering the freshman year of college. Increasingly, students stayed on to take advantage of the added training. In 1894 President Hutchinson reported to the Board of Trustees his assessment of the work of the school to date and of the future needs and possibilities.

> In a short time the institution has attained a secure place in the confidence of the people. Students come from every direction and they are as a class above the average in diligence and talent; many earn their own way by teaching or otherwise. . . . The Methodism and the people of West Virginia expect great things of the Conference Seminary during the next few years. All we need is the money to lead the educational work of the state. It has now become apparent to the faculty that we shall soon need to provide the full college course in order to hold what we gain and to secure the future of the school in competing with inferior schools calling themselves "College." The logic of the situation will compel us ere long to advance to the full college curriculum to which we are already much nearer than many suppose . . . I might name among our more pressing needs a gymnasium, large additions to our library and to the physical and chemical building or Science Hall, but above all, the ever present need of endowment.

President Hutchinson resigned his office at the end of the winter quarter of the 1897-98 school year and departed in February to assume the office of the president of the Genessee Wesleyan Seminary at Lima, New York. His resignation as president of the West Virginia Conference Seminary was in part due to the fact that the financial resources necessary for the development of full college rank for the school were not available. The Board of Trustees, upon his voluntary retirement from the institution,

37

caused the following resolution to be forwarded to Reverend Hutchinson and to be spread upon the minutes of the board for June 14, 1898:

> For eight years the Reverend B. W. Hutchinson, B.D., was principal of the West Virginia Conference Seminary of the Methodist Episcopal Church in this city. He came to the Seminary at its organization. He brought to this a disciplined mind, a good judgment, and a conscientious discharge of duty. Under his careful management the institution has steadily grown, has widened in influence, has risen in its requirement of scholarship until it ranks among the very best institutions of its character in the west and south. This growth and development has been the delight and the pride of the Methodist Episcopal Church of West Virginia, and to President Hutchinson this success is largely due and we take pleasure in giving him the proper credit for it.

Dr. Frank B. Trotter assumed the responsibility of acting president until the summer of 1898. Dr. Trotter (1863-1940), a native of Washington County, Ohio, came to West Virginia in his teens. At the age of twenty he was teaching in the public schools of Preston County. He graduated from Roanoke College in 1890 with an A.B. degree in the classics. During 1891-92 he attended Harvard University. He served as professor of Latin and modern languages at the seminary from 1890 to 1907. He was also vice president of the seminary. In this office he performed the functions of a dean. There is general agreement that Dr. Trotter was a bulwark of the school both as an administrator and as a teacher. Students of the seminary years still remember his appearances at the chapel service before each vacation period when he invariably urged them to go home and spread good news about the seminary. It has been observed that no student came to Dr. Trotter's class unprepared, if he could help it. He left the seminary in 1907 to become professor of Latin at West Virginia University. He was dean of the College of Arts and Sciences from 1911 to 1917. He was named acting president of the university in 1914. He served as president of the university from 1916 to 1928 when he returned to the classroom as professor of Latin.

Dr. Simon L. Boyers was elected to the presidency of the seminary in June 1898. A graduate of Ohio Wesleyan University and a Methodist minister, Dr. Boyers has been described as a gentleman whose educational and cultural experience, pleasant appearance and Christian character seemed to fit him admirably for the job. His administration of the affairs of the college, however, led to discussion at the end of his first year about whether or not he should be rehired. Dr. Haught recalls that in the spring of 1899 the president had almost the entire front of the campus planted in potatoes and oats. The venture came to an abrupt end at the hands of students who, under cover of darkness, used scythes to harvest the growing crops prematurely. One student involved in the escapade indicated that he rid himself of the temptation to swing the scythe only by yielding to the temptation. In November 1899, a Halloween prank on campus, which resulted in the accidental shooting of a student, brought an inquiry by the Board of Trustees into Dr. Boyers' administration. Serious concern was raised by the report that the president had authorized night watchmen to carry guns, and to shoot to protect the property of the school. The irate father of the wounded student who referred in the Board of Trustees meeting to the present "shotgun administration" threatened to sue the board. Dr. Boyers was absolved of responsibility for the shooting, but the incident had unhappy repercussions involving the charge that some students and faculty felt he was not a competent administrator. Dr. Boyers submitted his resignation as president on June 12, 1900.

In 1899 during Dr. Boyers' administration, the trustees of the seminary made plans to participate in the Twentieth Century Thank Offering of $20,000,000 proposed by the Bishops of the Methodist Church. The offering was part of a three-point program which included a call to Methodists to higher spiritual living and the conversion of two million souls to observe the ending of the nineteenth century and the advent of the twentieth century. The trustees and the presiding elders petitioned the West Virginia Annual Conference to share in the offering to the amount of $125,000. Of this amount they proposed that $20,000 be used to pay off the college's bonded indebtedness, that $5,000 be spent for improvements, and that $100,000 be set aside as endowment.

The Board of Trustees meeting on June 28, 1900, elected Dr. John Weir of Woodsfield, Ohio, as president of the seminary. Dr. Weir served in this capacity until September 1907. A Canadian by birth, he and Mrs. Weir had spent some years in Japan as missionaries. Before coming to the West Virginia Conference Seminary, he was president of Scio College in Ohio. Dr. Weir has been described as a tall, straight man with graying hair, dignified, kindly, a consummate optimist, fond of philosophy and the liberal use of hyperbole. Dr. Haught observes that Dr. Weir's vision of the potential of the school frequently blinded him to reality. He seemed not to know that adjectives and adverbs have positive and comparative degrees, for he used only the superlative degree. His vigor and optimism were put to good use.

One of Dr. Weir's major concerns from the beginning of his administration was the need for endowment. An appeal to the alumni of the school resulted in a pledge of $2,000 toward an endowment fund to be paid by January 1, 1903. In 1903 Dr. Weir reported to the Board of Trustees the result of a major effort to secure endowment funds during the preceding year. Through the assistance of Miss May G. Dolliver of Fort Dodge, Iowa, he had succeeded in eliciting a promise of a gift of $25,000 from Dr. D. K. Pearsons of Chicago, Illinois, provided the seminary would raise $75,000. He was allowed to count $15,000, the total amount raised by the Twentieth Century Thank Offering as part of the seminary's share. The result of the effort was the raising of a total of $100,000 endowment which, Dr. Weir noted in his report, stood second in total of endowments among all the seminaries in the country.

Early in Dr. Weir's administration the architect, Mr. Geisy, presented to the Board of Trustees plans drawn at the request of the executive committee for an addition to the Ladies' Hall and for a Conservatory of Music. It was not until the following year, 1902, that the board instructed the executive committee to proceed at once to erect a suitable building upon the campus to accommodate the Music Department and authorized a bond issue in the amount of $5,000 to cover its erection. The building, though not completed, was in use beginning January 1903, having been erected at a cost of approximately $6,500.

On February 4, 1905, the main seminary building was destroyed by fire which broke out in the basement in the vicinity of the furnaces. The combined efforts of students, faculty and citizens of Buckhannon saved the student records, books from the library, and most of the furniture. There were no serious accidents. President Weir was in Charleston meeting with leaders of the Senate on an education bill pending before the legislature when news of the fire came. He immediately communicated with the faculty and learned that under Dr. Trotter's leadership, plans had already been made for the continuance of school work without a break. Classes were distributed among the Music Hall, the parlors of the Ladies' Hall, and a vacant house on College Avenue.

The Board of Trustees met on February 15 to discuss the crisis created by the fire. Dr. Weir reported that he had communicated immediately with Dr. Pearsons and other wealthy men seeking contributions for the erection of a new building. Since February 5, over five thousand letters had gone out from this office soliciting funds. A signed statement advertising the fact that the school would continue to function had been sent to every newspaper in the state. The question before the trustees, he said, was to build or not to build. Not to build meant the abandonment of the educational work for which the seminary was founded. Dr. Weir even suggested that possibly the fire had been a blessing in disguise inasmuch as the school had grown too large already for the modest building in which it was housed. He reported that the insurance adjustors had estimated the sound value of the old building to be $29,000. It had been insured for $16,000, and he had been informed unofficially that it would be paid in full. To rebuild would require a major effort to raise funds. The trustees decided to rebuild. Professors Trotter, Mills and Haught, at the request of President Weir, made a rough draft of plans for a building to be submitted to an architect. From among the various architects who submitted proposals for the new building, the board selected the firm of Harding and Uphaus of Washington, D. C. A resolution authorized the executive committee and the architect to prepare plans and specifications for a new college building at Buckhannon which would cost, including a power plant, not more than $75,000, and to advertise for bids for the construction of the facilities at the earliest date possible.

When the trustees met again on March 9, President Weir reported that he had received many answers to his appeal for funds, but as yet no one had made a subscription. Bids were read for construction of the new building which ranged from a low of $57,255 to a high of $81,300. The bid of Ellicott and Winchell of Clarksburg, West Virginia, of $57,255 was accepted. A building committee was appointed consisting of Professors Frank B. Trotter and W. O. Mills, representing the faculty; Robert A. Reger, D. A. Denton, C. B. Graham, John Weir, and A. M. Poundstone representing the Board of Trustees. The building was subsequently erected by Withrow and Company of Charleston, West Virginia, on a contract of $61,249. The power house was erected by Post, Martin and Company of Buckhannon on a contract of $3,100.40. Several substantial contributions were made by Dr. D. K. Pearsons of Chicago in the amount of $10,000; Andrew Carnegie, $18,000; and a trustee, John Archbold of New York, $5,000. The building was completed in 1906 at a cost of $60,000. Other improvements including the power house were made at a cost of $10,000.

As significant for the future of the school as anything which transpired during Dr. Weir's administration was the raising of the seminary to full college work. In 1892 an extra year of work had been added. As early as 1893-94, President Hutchinson had noted that it was apparent that soon a full college course should be provided. Increasingly, graduates of the seminary stayed on to do advanced work. In 1901 President Weir recommended to the Board of Trustees the addition of another year to the course of study and the adoption of a resolution which would permit the initiation of college work at the earliest possible moment. Both items were approved. In June 1903, the situation had developed to the extent that Dr. Weir reported to the trustees:

> I believe the time has come for extension of our courses of study. We need only two years more to reach the full college course. We have gone too far to go back. We should complete the college work. We ought not to change our institution into a college. We should hold to our preparatory work and improve it, hold to our seminary work and improve it, then add to the college work. We should give diplomas in the seminary courses just as we grant degrees in college courses. I would recommend the following: that we, this coming autumn, extend our college work to full college and that we do not change the name of our school until we are recognized as a college by the University Senate of the Church.

The school offered work of full college grade beginning in the fall of 1903, with an A.B. degree granted following the Seminary Classical Course, the B.S. degree following the Seminary Scientific Course, and the B.Litt. degree following the Seminary Literary Course. The catalogue announced that the seminary course as printed satisfied the requirements of the University Senate of the Methodist Episcopal Church and left ten courses as a surplus to be counted as college work. A course was a class which met five times per week for one term. Thirty-eight additional courses, thirty-two required and six elective, constituted work for the various degrees. In April 1904, President Weir reported to the Board of Trustees:

> Four years ago we began college classes. We have proceeded cautiously. We have yielded to demands naturally created. We did not set up artificial demands. Quietly, successfully we have proceeded; and next year, 1905, our first gowned college class will graduate. Our college courses accord with those prescribed and required by the University Senate of our Church. They are those of the best colleges. Our college work displaces none of the Seminary preparatory or departmental work. It fosters all. We have proceeded under the order and sanction of this Board and now we ask that you give us a name in agreement with our broader character.

42

After considering such names as Epworth University, Batelle University, Methodist University of West Virginia, Wesley College, College of West Virginia, West Virginia College, and West Virginia Wesleyan University, the board finally decided upon the Wesleyan University of West Virginia.

The annual conference Committee on Education reported to the conference in 1904:

> Of the fifty-two schools of Seminary grade in The Methodist Episcopal Church in the world, our school in West Virginia ranks fourth in value of buildings and grounds and second in amount of endowment. We have raised more for endowment during the quadrennium than any other seminary in the Church save one.

The annual conference passed a resolution approving the action of the Board of Trustees in raising the school to college grade and requested the Board of Education of the Methodist Episcopal Church to approve the development and insert the school in its list of approved colleges. In June 1906, the trustees voted unanimously to change the name of the school to West Virginia Wesleyan College.

When the institution was raised to full college grade, the seminary was continued, but the work was cut back to three years. From 1906 through the spring of 1908, the term "seminary" was replaced by the designation "Preparatory Department." The last class in the seminary was graduated in 1908. From 1908 until its demise the work of the old seminary was continued as the "Academic Department" or "Academy." By 1922-23 the need for the work of the academy had passed with the growth of high schools in the state and the academy was discontinued. A few sub-freshman courses were provided for those not adequately prepared for college work. In 1924 these vestigial remains of the old seminary disappeared, and the summer school was advertised as offering work for those not fully prepared for college courses.

Despite the success in raising endowment funds deficits began to accumulate each year so that during the years 1900-06 the Board of Trustees ascertained that the accumulated annual deficit of expenses over income, plus money owed the president, plus money borrowed from the Endowment Fund to meet current expenses, amounted to a total of $24,365.17. By the spring meeting of the board in 1907, the deficit had risen to $31,420.82. The treasurer of the board reported that interest on money borrowed for current expenses was draining the treasury, and that he had been forced to set aside $1,600 of the Andrew Carnegie gift for the

43

rebuilding of Main Hall to pay off said interest. An alarmed board authorized the finance committee to borrow $35,000 to be secured by college property and endowment funds in order to retire the deficit. Within a month this amount had to be increased to $42,500. The president of the college and the executive committee were urged to seek ways to eliminate all possible expense without serious embarrassment to the institution.

The problems of the school were compounded when at the same meeting President Weir submitted his resignation. Before a new president could be secured, Dr. Trotter also resigned.

On June 12, 1907, the Board of Trustees elected Dr. Carl G. Doney to the presidency of the college. At the same time, it acted to do away with the office of vice president and elected to the deanship the Reverend Dr. W. A. Haggarty, who served in this capacity until 1909.

Dr. Doney, a native of Ohio, came to Wesleyan after having tried briefly a career in law and then the ministry. He served churches in Ohio and came to Wesleyan from the Hamline Methodist Church in Washington, D. C.

Writing his autobiography in 1942, Dr. Doney said that the Wesleyan he found when he arrived in Buckhannon in September 1907, would scarcely now be ranked as a college.[1] The main buildings were in good shape, but the library and laboratory were poorly housed and furnished. The official most responsible for Dr. Doney's election as president had made professors out of several of his friends, but they proved to be round pegs in square holes. An immediate necessity was the rebuilding of the faculty.

Of prime concern to Dr. Doney was the low financial state of affairs which he inherited. Even before coming to Wesleyan, Dr. Doney notes that he had a conversation with himself regarding the school which came to this conclusion:

> West Virginia needs a religious college; this school is well located; it should have an excellent faculty, proper equipment, and high standards; to achieve these ends, money will be required for buildings, furnishings, and teachers; the people have the money; they need only to be told of this great opportunity and they will give the money; I will tell them about it in city and country and come back with pockets full. . . . I had forgotten that a juryman never votes a verdict that will cost him money, or that no one pays money just because it is the logical thing to do.

[1] Carl G. Doney, *Cheerful Yesterdays and Confident Tomorrows* (Portland, Oregon: Binfords and Mort, 1942).

A request by Dr. Doney early in his administration for an appraisal of the value of college property brought the following report from the committee of the trustees appointed to make the valuation: 43 acres college campus, $65,000; College Hall, $80,000; Music Hall, $6,000; Ladies' Hall, $20,000; Heating and Power Plant, $10,000, and President's Residence, $2,500, for a total of $183,500. The endowment helped increase the assets to approximately $250,000. But, Dr. Doney noted, the endowment fund which approached $100,000 was offset by a debt that approximated the same amount. More money and more students were required if the school were not to fail. A decline in enrollment had set in at the turn of the century coincident with the program of high school building in the state.

Dr. Doney discovered that churches were always open to him, but appeals to logic and feeling brought little financial return and few students. Operating on the theory that an informed constituency would respond to the need of the school, Dr. Doney acquired a small printing press, taught students to operate it and began to send bulletins to high schools, churches and a large group of individuals. A committee was appointed by the trustees to plan and institute a campaign to lift the debt on the college and to increase the endowment to $200,000. A financial agent was placed in the field.

The concerted and continuous effort to increase the income of the school and the size of the student body subsequently bore fruit. Dr. Doney reported that at the end of eight years the debt had been paid and the endowment increased. However, yearly deficits continued to harass the school. When Dr. Doney resigned as president of the college, a report of the auditing committee showed that the assets of the college had been increased to $445,162.21. Liabilities amounted to $69,459.36. An attempt instituted in 1910 to increase the endowment fund failed as did a plan projected in 1912 to raise an endowment fund of $250,000. Small yearly amounts were added to the fund so that by the time of Dr. Doney's resignation as president, the audit committee reported an endowment of $123,000.

Part of the increase in assets came from the value of two buildings erected during Dr. Doney's tenure as president. On April 25, 1912, the Executive Committee of the Board of Trustees authorized the erection of a gymnasium when available funds for that purpose should reach $10,000. The gymnasium was erected in 1912, and facilities were completed the following year with a gift of $5,000 from Colonel Seymour Edwards conditioned by the school's raising a like amount.

Construction on the Haymond Science Hall was begun in 1913, and the building was completed and occupied early in the spring of 1914. The building and furnishings were the gift of Mrs. Virginia Haymond in memory of her husband Colonel Sydney Haymond who served on the Board of Trustees from 1906-12. Mrs. Haymond succeeded her husband as a trustee and served until her death in 1917.

A decisive event in the life of Wesleyan came during Dr. Doney's administration with the election in 1909 of Thomas W. Haught as dean of the college.

Thomas W. Haught (1871-1957), a native of Tyler County, West Virginia, came to the new seminary at Buckhannon in March 1891. He completed the Classical Course in 1894 and finished work for the Bachelor of Arts degree in June 1896, at West Virginia University. He subsequently attended Harvard University from 1899 to 1901 for graduate study.

His relationship to Wesleyan as a teacher and administrator was to cover a period of forty years. He served on the faculty under every president from Dr. Bennett W. Hutchinson to Dr. Joseph W. Broyles. He was emeritus professor into the administration of Dr. Stanley H. Martin. He taught science, English and mathematics at the seminary from 1896-99, and again from 1901-05. After three years as president of the State School at Keyser, West Virginia, now known as Potomac State College, he returned to Wesleyan in 1908. He became the second dean of the college in 1909 and occupied this post for twenty years. During these years he served as acting president of Wesleyan in 1913, 1922 and 1925. He served on the West Virginia State Board of Education from 1910 to 1920. Wesleyan awarded Dean Haught an honorary Master of Arts degree in 1916. In 1929 he resigned as dean to teach geology. Wesleyan conferred on him the honorary degree of Doctor of Science.

Dean Haught's history of Wesleyan, *West Virginia Wesleyan College, 1890-1940,* was published on the occasion of the fiftieth anniversary of the school. Dean Haught retired in 1941. He served as chairman of the Charles W. Gibson Library from 1941 to 1953. In 1950 he published in mimeograph form *The Sixth Decade, 1940-1950,* a supplement to his history of Wesleyan. He assisted with the publication of the 1947 Alumni Directory, and served as the first president of the Alumni Fund Board of Directors. In 1950 the Alumni Association presented him with the Alumni Award for outstanding loyalty and devotion to Wesleyan.

Dean Haught was known as a firm disciplinarian, capable of sharp and caustic rebuke for those who flouted college regulations. He had a reputation as a thorough and intelligent scholar, qualities which he also displayed in his teaching. As dean he pressed for the recognition of Wesleyan by the North Central Association of Colleges and Secondary Schools, and he has been given much of the credit for the final achievement of this goal in 1927. In the opinion of those who knew him and his work, no individual has made a greater contribution to the life of Wesleyan than Dean Thomas W. Haught.

Other developments of less spectacular nature but nonetheless important to the physical and academic well-being of the school occurred during Doney's presidency. Cement walks from the three principle entrances to the campus to College Hall and the Ladies' Hall replaced old board walks. The Harmer Gateway and the Atkinson Gateway were constructed. The Memorial Gate at the southwest entrance to the campus was donated by the Normal Class of 1913. Board fences along College Avenue and Meade Street, constructed during the early years to keep domestic animals off the campus, were removed.

Beginning June 1910, teachers were ranked for the first time according to their work and salary. Heads of departments were designated "professors." Those who were not department heads but taught full time were designated "instructors." Salaries for a full professor were to be not less than $1,000 for a man and $750 for a woman. Assistant professors were to receive not less than $500.

The Board of Trustees took action necessary to the granting of honorary degrees and the first degrees were bestowed in 1912 on the Reverend George Dolliver Smith (D.D.), the Honorable Henry Clay McWhorter (L.L.D.), and the Honorable William Seymour Edwards (Litt.D.).

In 1914 the trustees established the Chair of Bible and Philosophy with the Reverend Richard Aspinall the first to occupy the position.

At the close of the basketball season in 1914, on the initiative of Harry Stansbury, Director of Athletics, the two leading high school teams in the state, Wheeling and Elkins, were invited to play for the state championship at Wesleyan. The following season invitations were extended to all high schools wishing to participate. Thus began the state high school basketball tournament which was held at Wesleyan until 1938 when it was moved to Morgantown. Within a few years after its inauguration the number of teams participating in the tournament exceeded sixty. To accommodate the tournament which ran for three days, the gymnasium was enlarged during the school year 1920-21, so that the length of the playing floor was doubled. The games were played two at a time. Eventually the State High School Athletic Association held sectional tournaments which cut down on the number of teams participating in the event at Wesleyan.

Student life at Wesleyan during the early years has been termed "strict." Mr. Roy Reger of Buckhannon, the first student to enroll in the seminary, later recorded his memories of this era. He noted that the students, who were nearly all from West Virginia, had little money. Some cooked their own meals, some took their meals in private boarding houses. Those who lived within traveling distance of Buckhannon went home on weekends and brought back enough food to last for two or three days. Furniture was scarce. Chairs were carried from one room to another for large gatherings. When a piano was needed for a program on the second floor of the seminary building, students carried one down from the third floor and then returned it after the program. The bell in the tower of the seminary building rang loud and long at 7:00 o'clock each evening to warn students to be off the street and in their rooms for study. Daily chapel attendance was compulsory and the roll of students was called at each session. Church attendance on Sunday was mandatory, and at the roll call for Monday Chapel each student was required to answer "church" or "not at church." Social life centered largely in two literary societies.

A list of "requirements" and "prohibitions" was published in 1892, composed of regulations found necessary for proper discipline. While self-control was the ideal held up to the students, it was suggested that cheerful obedience to rules, promptness in the discharge of duty, and proper reverence for superiors were necessary to the formation of the best type of character. Ladies and gentlemen, except brothers and sisters, were not allowed to occupy rooms in the same house. Permission of the president was required for students to leave town or sever their connection with the seminary, and for the literary societies and all public exercises to meet after 10:00 o'clock p.m. Faculty permission was required to take up or drop a study, and to engage board and room at hotels. Students were cautioned against incurring debts for merchandise, room and board.

Young ladies were not allowed to be away from their boarding houses in the evening without permission, nor were they allowed to receive gentleman callers any evening except Saturday, and then only such as were approved by the faculty or the preceptress. They were not permitted to receive young men or to go walking with them on the Sabbath. Students were prohibited from taking excursions by land or water, attending fairs, sociables or entertainments without permission; lounging about stores, streets, depots or any other public places; attending balls, dances or theatres. The use of tobacco in the buildings or on the campus was prohibited, and the use of intoxicating liquors by students was absolutely prohibited. Graduates who were students when the no-smoking rule was in force recall that some students and faculty would dash madly off the campus limits to have a quick smoke between classes. Parents were advised not to send students boxes of confectionery or edibles of any kind. They were informed also that outside of the regular expenses of the school, there was little need of pocket money, and they would do their children a service by requiring an itemized account of all expenses.

The center of social life recalled by Mr. Reger was the Chrestomathean and the Excelsior Literary Societies. These societies were organized soon after opening of the first term by the simple device of dividing the roster of students into two groups, equal in number, and appointing faculty members to advise and guide each group. The students organized by adopting names and constitutions and by electing officers. Each society had its own "hall," and great care was exercised in furnishing and decorating the room. The society meetings were the chief social event of the week and one of the few opportunities for the mingling of the sexes in a social setting. The program for an evening consisted of music, prayer, business, the reading of poetry, declamations, essays, orations. The main event of the evening was a debate followed by an announcement of the winner by judges appointed early in the meeting and remarks on the debate by a critic who was one of the elected officers of the society. Debates covered a variety of subjects including women suffrage, politics, religion, the use of tobacco and liquor, science, war—the whole gamut of human and contemporary concern. During the spring term the two societies met in a joint contest. The contests would fill the chapel to its capacity of nearly a thousand, but the rivalry became so intense that they were prohibited by the faculty within a few years after the societies were established.

Information regarding athletics during the early years of the seminary is fragmentary. Dr. Haught recalls that though much of the school ground was reserved for a cow pasture, groups of students would play baseball at the southwest corner of the campus where trees were scarce. After the erection of the Ladies' Hall, a tennis court was constructed near the hall and adjacent to Meade Street. Before the fire which destroyed the original building, basketball was organized and games were played on the third floor of the building. These sports, except perhaps for an occasional basketball game, were intramural.

The first football game played by a seminary team, and the first to be played in Upshur County, was in 1898. Henry White, the star of the team, arranged the game with a group of ex-college men located in Buckhannon, serving as civil engineers in the building of the Baltimore and Ohio Railroad. The game was played on a snowy, bitterly cold day. Neither team made a touchdown, but the B. and O. Engineers claimed victory for having scored a safety. After some argument, the game was declared a draw.[2]

Wesleyan's orange and black colors date back to that first football game. Colonel Frank M. Thompson, fullback and captain of the team, idealized the Poe brothers, football greats at Princeton University. Thompson played the first game garbed in an orange and black turtle-necked sweater like the sweaters worn by the Poe brothers. When his teammates admired the sweater, Thompson announced that orange and black would be their official colors. When athletics were formally recognized by the school, the precedent was continued and became fixed.

The Board of Trustees acted favorably on a petition presented to it in the spring of 1899, containing eighty-four student signatures, requesting the appropriation of one hundred dollars for baseball equipment and a diamond to be ready for use at the opening of the next school year.

It was not until 1902 that athletics gained the formal recognition of the school. The September issue of the *Seminary Collegiate* indicated that this had been a red letter day at the college. The president had extended the chapel hour for a meeting of the student body to perfect the organization of an athletic association. A constitution and by-laws were adopted. The *Collegiate* went on to note that Coach Peck felt the school had good material for a football team, that arrangements were being made to have

---

[2] Kent Kessler, *Hail West Virginians!* (Parkersburg, W. Va.: Park Press, 1959), p. 129.

a baseball coach in the near future. Basketball and gymnastics were already in progress.

Wesleyan's first official football team made its appearance in 1902. Ed Kenna, who had made a name for himself at Georgetown University and West Virginia University, was the coach.

The first mention of athletics in the catalogue of the school came in 1905 with the publication of eight eligibility requirements and prohibitions to be observed by students who were participants in the athletic program. The catalogue of 1908 noted that an athletic program had been established based on the premise that since a sound body is essential to the highest efficiency in scholarship, athletic exercise has a proper place in college life.

Once it was established as a sport, feelings regarding football sometimes rose to spirited heights. For example, the 1905 season was short-lived. The schedule was cancelled following victories in the first three games, ostensibly because some Wesleyan boys were playing contrary to eligibility rules. The real trouble appears to have involved friction between President Weir and the student body which resulted from his critical remarks concerning some members of the football team whom he referred to as "roughnecks." He also had identified as a model student a young man who wore his hair long and spoke in a high-pitched tone. The young man's locks were shorn by a group of students. President Weir cancelled the schedule because some football players had been involved in the incident. Students held a mass meeting to protest the cancellation. They burned the president in effigy. They stole his cow and placed it on the chapel rostrum. Nevertheless, the schedule remained cancelled.

From 1892-94 President Hutchinson periodically issued a small news bulletin under the title of *The Seminary Herald*. During the school year 1899-1900 two students, W. H. Franklin and C. H. King, began monthly publication of a small magazine-type paper known as *The Seminary Collegiate*. In 1904-05 the managing editor of the *Collegiate* asked the help of the faculty in selecting a name for the school paper from three which had been suggested. The name *Pharos* was chosen. The new paper was published weekly. Around 1907 the *Pharos* offered a lifetime subscription to any student writing the most acceptable college song. George N. Steyer of the class of 1909 won the subscription with a poem bearing the name of the school and set to the tune of "Maryland My Maryland":

51

We raise our voice in song to thee,
  West Virginia Wesleyan.
O, may we ever loyal be,
  West Virginia Wesleyan.
We love our state, her wooded hills,
Her mountain streams and gushing rills
But thou our heart with rapture thrills,
  West Virginia Wesleyan.

Proud sons and daughters boast of thee,
  West Virginia Wesleyan.
Thine is a precious history,
  West Virginia Wesleyan.
Yet we in thought and purpose one
Pursue thy work so well begun,
  Our school shall never be outdone,
  West Virginia Wesleyan.

May length of years upon thee wait,
  West Virginia Wesleyan.
May we, thy children, make thee great,
  West Virginia Wesleyan.
We shout our motto loud and long
"Up with the right, down with the wrong,"
O, now accept our humble song,
  West Virginia Wesleyan.

The first school annual was published in May 1903, by the students of the seminary class of 1904. Dr. Haught believes that the name *Murmurmontis* was suggested by Dr. Trotter. A rough translation of the word is "The voice of the mountain."

The earliest group on campus with a specific religious purpose was a periodic meeting of pre-ministerial students with President Hutchinson to discuss facets of their future work. The existence of the group was first mentioned in the catalogue for 1894-95; and when the first *Murmurmontis* was published, the name of the organization was listed as "The Epworth Ministerial Association." The YWCA was organized in 1900 and the YMCA the following year.

As early as the first commencement President Hutchinson held a "Commencement love feast" on baccalaureate Sunday afternoon. The service consisted of congregational singing, voluntary prayers and the relating of personal religious experience. The love feast was well attended during the first ten years of the life of the school, but declining attendance ultimately forced the discontinuing of the practice. Another service inaugurated during the first years was a weekly Sunday afternoon students' meeting which stressed Bible study and serious discussion of the religious life. The meetings were generally conducted by President Hutchinson with an occasional assist by faculty members. Attendance was voluntary and good for the first two decades, but again declining interest forced the abandonment of the practice.

The imminent completion of the Ladies' Hall during the summer of 1895 motivated a group of women in Buckhannon to meet informally to sew sheets, pillowcases and other accessories for the new dormitory. Out of this group came the organization known as the College Club. The first mention of the group appeared in the minutes of the Board of Trustees in the spring of 1909 in a resolution expressing appreciation for the work of the club in providing furnishings and equipment for the dormitory. The College Club still functions and lends material assistance to the college.

On June 14, 1915, Dr. Doney tendered his resignation to the Board of Trustees and left to become president of Willamette University. The end of his tenure as president also marked the 25th anniversary of the school. In a twenty-five year period it had expanded from a seminary of high school grade to a four-year college. In 1915 the college granted 108 degrees, certificates and diplomas in comparison with the five who graduated in the first class of the seminary. The physical plant had grown from a single building and grounds costing about $38,500 to five college buildings and a residence for the president valued along with grounds and equipment at $270,654.58. Its endowment was less than half this amount and its indebtedness and other liabilities were equal to almost half the endowment. For most of its years the school had been harassed by financial problems. At the end of twenty-five years the official annual conference visitor to the college reported, "Undoubtedly the incubus on the college is financial."

III

STRUGGLE FOR SURVIVAL

The Board of Trustees meeting August 12, 1915, in Clarksburg, nominated Dr. Wallace B. Fleming of Drew Theological Seminary to succeed Dr. Doney.

Dr. Wallace B. Fleming was born November 22, 1872, near Newark, Ohio. He received the A.B. degree at Muskingum College, Ohio, the B.D. degree at Drew University and the Ph.D. degree at Columbia University. From 1897 to 1911 he served as pastor of churches successively at North Patterson, Bayonne and Maplewood, New Jersey. He came to West Virginia Wesleyan College after having served as professor of Greek and Hebrew and as registrar at Drew Theological Seminary.

It is generally agreed that the promotion of the material interests of the college is the accomplishment for which Dr. Fleming's administration has been most favorably remembered. In June of 1915, the trustees had voted to concur in the jubilee campaign for an educational forward movement throughout the Methodist Episcopal Church to begin the first of December. Upon recommendation of Dr. Fleming and the Committee on Endowment the trustees meeting in June 1916 voted to join in the general jubilee campaign with the determination to add one-half million dollars to the resources of the college within the next two years. Of this amount, $400,000 was earmarked for the permanent endowment fund, and the remaining $100,000 was designated a contingent fund to pay all outstanding indebtedness and to provide for the deficit of the institution.

One year later the Board of Trustees met at the college to be present for the final phase of the Half Million Fund Campaign which had been telescoped into one year. On the morning of June 6, a bulletin board in the hall of the main college building showed that $448,000 had been raised. At 10:00 o'clock a.m. a telegram from Charleston raised the total to $458,000 and by noon it was $461,000. The afternoon meeting of the board recessed until 7:00 o'clock p.m. to meet at the courthouse with the people of Buckhannon who had been invited to assist in raising the balance of $31,275. At 8:00 o'clock p.m. Dr. Fleming announced to a crowd which filled the courtroom that he assumed at least $3,500 would be

54

received over the wires during the evening leaving a balance of $27,775 to raise. Committees were appointed to solicit new subscriptions, and additions to those already made, from the audience. At 10:00 o'clock Dr. Fleming announced that the full amount of $500,000 and more had been subscribed. The news was greeted with "the beating of drums, the blowing of horns, huzzas, and general rejoicing," with a bonfire on campus around which students and the general public joined.

Despite the success of the campaign, the college continued to grapple with the problem of finances. Pledges were difficult to collect and there was the inevitable shrinkage in pledges accentuated by the fluctuating economic situation of the years of World War I. In 1919 the trustees accepted a proposition from the General Education Board of New York (The Rockefeller Fund) to pay the college the sum of $125,000 provided that it raise an additional sum of money in the amount of $375,000. The Rockefeller Fund agreed to pay $1 for each $3 raised by the college. The effort to raise the college's share of the proposition was known as the Victory Fund. In June 1926, Dr. Fleming reported to the trustees that the last payments on the Half Million Fund would be due October 1. He suggested that a conference-wide canvass be made to continue annual giving for three more years to a Victory Fund. How successful this attempt was is not indicated. The Rockefeller Fund granted successive extensions of the deadline for the raising of the college share, and as late as 1930 the trustees were still trying to raise money in order to claim the last $20,000 increment.

In 1922 Dr. Fleming proposed a campaign among friends of the college and the West Virginia Annual Conference for not less than $1,500,000 to provide the buildings and endowment necessary to care adequately for the near-future needs of the institution. The proposed campaign never got off the ground.

The entrance of the United States into World War I brought to the campus a Student Army Training Corps of about 200 men. The military training program which was to have begun September 1, 1918, actually ran only from the beginning of October to the early days of December. The corps was housed in the gymnasium. The Music Hall was converted to a hospital to care for members of the corps who were stricken during the influenza epidemic.

The steady growth of the student body following the war raised the issue of the expansion of the physical plant of the college with emphasis

55

on the need for additional living space for women, quarters for professors, a library, and the enlargement of the gymnasium. The only building project completed during Dr. Fleming's administration, however, was the expansion of the gymnasium during the school year 1920-21.

By action of the trustees on June 7, 1920, the women's dormitory which had been dubbed unofficially "The Ladies' Hall" was named Agnes Howard Hall in memory of the daughter of Mr. C. D. Howard who had contributed substantially to the erection of the building. Miss Howard had died while a student at Wesleyan.

The year 1920 also marked the inauguration of a program designed to serve the church. Under the leadership of the Reverend Mr. Aaron Rapking, a Department of Rural Leadership was established, jointly sponsored by the college and by the Rural Department of the Board of Home Missions and Church Extension of the Methodist Episcopal Church. The purpose of the department was to provide courses in rural sociology, rural economics, and rural leadership which would train ministers, teachers and laymen to assume leadership and render Christian services in the small town and open country. The following year courses in religious education were added. By 1922 there was a separate Department of Religious Education. By 1927 the two departments had been combined. The program ceased to function at the end of the school year.

The Department of Rural Leadership conducted such extension work as surveys of parishes and districts, supervision of student pastors, vacation church schools, help to churches in planning community projects, furnishing of plans for rural churches and community houses, and mailing books from the college library to rural ministers.

Early in 1922 Dr. Fleming announced the gift of $4,000 by Mr. George W. Atkinson, a past governor of West Virginia and a member of the Board of Trustees, $3,000 of which was to be applied to the purchase of a pipe organ for the chapel. By action of the trustees the chapel in the Administration Building was named Atkinson Chapel in recognition of Mr. Atkinson's service to the college and of his public service.

Although the trustees of the college had organized themselves into a corporation in 1888, it was deemed necessary to incorporate the college under the provisions of a law passed by the state legislature in 1919. A committee composed of W. W. Hughes, Samuel V. Woods, U. G. Young, and C. W. Lynch prepared the necessary papers for incorporation. In June 1920 the trustees adopted a Certificate of Incorporation or Charter issued by Houston G. Young, secretary of state of West Virginia. By-laws were presented and adopted and a resolution was passed which transferred the control and direction of the college from the old trustees to the corporation established by the new charter.

Athletics at Wesleyan also received the attention of the Board of Trustees and Dr. Fleming. In his report to the trustees for June 1921, the president noted an increase in the debt of the Athletic Association from $7,000 reported the previous year, and suggested that athletic affairs be conducted by a committee directly responsible to the faculty. The following year he again noted the continuing financial difficulties of the association. Pursuant to his recommendations a special committee of the board chaired by Dr. Roy McCuskey studied the issue and on June 5, 1922, recommended the establishment of an organization to be called the Alumni Athletic Board of West Virginia Wesleyan College. The board would be composed of nine members, all of whom should be members of the Alumni Association, with the faculty, the trustees, the student body and alumni at large represented. The president of the Alumni Association, with the advice and consent of the president of the college, was given the responsibility for the annual appointment of these members. The duties of the board included encouraging clean athletics and the raising of funds sufficient to guarantee the school a proper place in the field of intercollegiate athletic competition. The board was charged with reporting to the trustees annually a complete statement of any indebtedness incurred during the year for which the college was responsible. The board could not encroach on the authority of the trustees or the faculty in the selection of coaches and managers or in the arranging of schedules.

This situation developed during a period dating from about 1915 to the early thirties when football at Wesleyan, as well as at other schools, was in the ascendency and some of Wesleyan's "greats" were making history in sports competition.

In 1916 Earle "Greasy" Neale returned to Wesleyan as football coach and remained through the following season. Neale, along with Harry Stansbury who became Director of Athletics at Wesleyan, had starred on the undefeated team of 1912. Neale joined the Cincinnati Reds baseball team in 1917 and played with the team in the World Series of 1919. He subsequently coached the Washington and Jefferson College football team to a Rose Bowl tie with the University of California, and as coach of the Philadelphia Eagles, professional football team, led his team to professional football championships in 1948 and 1949.

In 1924 the Wesleyan football team coached by Bob Higgins lost only two games, to West Virginia University and Waynesburg College. Nine victories included a 7 to 3 win over Syracuse University and a 24 to 7 win over Kentucky University. Wesleyan was invited to meet Southern Methodist University in a post-season game in Dallas, Texas, the forerunner of the present Sugar Bowl game. Wesleyan defeated S.M.U. by a score of 9 to 7.

In 1925 Cecil B. "Cebe" Ross became head football coach at Wesleyan. Under his coaching Wesleyan played and defeated New York University, West Virginia University, Navy, Kentucky University, and Duquesne University. Outstanding players coached by "Cebe" during his twenty-two seasons at Wesleyan included David Reemsnyder, later head coach and presently director of athletics; Leonard Barnum; Gale Bullman; Nelson Peterson; the Bachtel brothers, Forrest, Arthur, Howard and Ray; and Clifford "Cliff" Battles. Reemsnyder was named to the little All-American team. Battles, after a record-setting career in professional football, was elected to the National Football Hall of Fame on October 29, 1955.

This era came to an end during the early thirties. The growth of athletic conferences, national and regional, to deal with some of the pressing problems of intercollegiate football which had brought the game under attack from many quarters, brought about some adjustments in the program. Since the formation of the West Virginia Intercollegiate Athletic Conference in 1924, Wesleyan has participated in all phases of athletics within the framework of this conference and the small state and private colleges within West Virginia.

On July 18, 1922, Dr. Fleming accepted a call to the presidency of Baker University. His resignation was formally recognized by the Board of Trustees at the February 1923 meeting. A resolution by the trustees formally accepting Dr. Fleming's resignation noted that while his tenure at Wesleyan had not been long, "yet he crowded into it such great development for the permanent good of the College that we, its trustees, can cheerfully assert that he performed a well-founded work which might have required a less resourceful and devoted man many more years in its accomplishment." D. L. Ash, Archbold Moore and W. B. Mathews, a committee constituted to recommend applicants for the presidency, proposed five names for consideration at the April meeting of the trustees. Among the candidates were the Reverend Dr. C. Fred Anderson and the Reverend Dr. Roy McCuskey of the West Virginia Annual Conference of the Methodist Episcopal Church. The nomination of these two individuals reflected a growing sentiment that a member of the West Virginia Annual Conference should be president of the school. However, by unanimous agreement the Reverend Dr. E. Guy Cutshall of Philadelphia, Pennsylvania, was selected as the new president.

From Dr. Fleming's departure until the inauguration of the new president, Dr. Thomas Haught was pressed into service as acting president. During the year Dr. Haught organized a student council of nine representatives from the four college classes and a president elected by the student body from the senior class. The council assumed no disciplinary function, but Dr. Haught noted that it promoted better morale in the school community. A committee of students and faculty was also organized to coordinate mutual concern for high standards of scholarship.

Dr. Cutshall's first report to the Board of Trustees, February 7, 1924, indicated that he had two major concerns. First, he wanted to protect the enrollment which had been increasing over the past ten years and to improve the quality of academic work. He suggested that an aggressive policy was needed by the college to enlarge and cultivate the student field in view of the competition of a strong state university, the conversion of a half dozen normal schools into state colleges, the loyalty of the northern panhandle to Ohio Wesleyan, the rapid development of Marshall College, and the existence in the state of five other colleges. Second, he voiced concern for the financial foundations of the college. From 1917 until 1923 the college had been run on a deficit in the aggregate of $123,674.15 for the six-year period. Deficits had been made up by borrowing from the endowment fund. The amount of $300,000 remained uncollected on the Half Million Fund. Students were in debt to the college for tuition and incidentals for the current year in the amount of $5,024.60.

Over the two-year period of his presidency Dr. Cutshall worked toward the improvement of the college's position on both these concerns. The Ray Collection Agency of Wheeling, West Virginia, was employed to collect subscriptions on the Half Million Fund, excepting the larger subscriptions and those subscribers in centers of population easily reached by a representative of the college. Tuition was increased from $50 to $60

59

per semester and a policy was adopted requiring payment of tuition in full before enrollment in the classes. Members of the administration and trustees were charged with the responsibility of finding 200 persons willing to give $100 per year each for five years to the current expense account.

In his final report to the Board of Trustees Dr. Cutshall reported on the accomplishments of his administration. Collections on the Half Million Fund and the Victory Fund had amounted to about $140,000; $49,000 had been received from the General Education Board; $19,000 on the drive to prevent a deficit for the school year 1923-24; $48,000 in gifts, wills and annuities. Economies in the operation of the school had resulted in savings amounting to about $6,400. Twelve new scholarships were added and students were currently realizing about $10,000 per year from scholarships and self-help employment in the college. Deputation work in the search for students was being done gratis by members of the student body. Improvements had been made on the gymnasium, the Administration Building, Science Hall and Agnes Howard Hall. A residence for the president on the corner of Sedgwick Street and College Avenue had been purchased at a cost of $10,000. The faculty had been strengthened by the addition of a number of new teachers including George Glauner and J. J. Bos. The faculty had adopted and put in force strict faculty regulations in matters of class attendance, tardiness, uniformity in grading, hours of required work, integrity in examinations. Student government had become a reality beginning with the second semester 1923-24 by the establishment of the Student Representative Council with power to enforce rules regulating the conduct of students in examinations, proper use of school property and the practice of good campus form. The system of weighted credits had been adopted which put the graduation requirements upon a qualitative as well as a quantitative basis. The curriculum committee and the faculty had instituted reforms which were designed to keep the offerings of the college up to date with the range of subjects adequate to and in harmony with the best standards. These involved the upgrading of requirements for graduation in psychology, physical education, fine arts, the sciences, foreign languages, business administration, and the Normal School. Wesleyan, according to Dr. Cutshall, had achieved a "first" in the state by adding courses in 1924 for the training of men and women for coaching. Professor Hyma had been instrumental in introducing intramural sports.

In a resolution of appreciation tendered Dr. Cutshall, the Board of

60

Trustees noted that he had given to all "a broader vision of college affairs . . . raised the standard of college work, strengthening and adding new courses . . . increased the salaries of the faculty . . . collected and added to our endowment, from old and new pledges, approximately $175,000. . . ." Dr. Cutshall left Wesleyan to become president of Iliff Seminary, Denver, Colorado. Later he served as president of Nebraska Wesleyan.

Dean Haught was again called to serve as acting president from June 1925, to the summer of 1926. He notes that during this period Dr. Lewis Chrisman became acting dean leaving him free to consider some problems of administration. The most outstanding among these was the abortive effort to secure recognition for the college by the North Central Association of Colleges and Secondary Schools. Pressure for several years from alumni who found themselves at a disadvantage in the teaching profession or in attempting to pursue graduate studies because the college had not been accredited by a standardizing agency led to the application for admission to the North Central Association of Colleges at its meeting in Chicago during March 1926. The application was rejected by the association after President R. M. Hughes of Miami University reported on his inspection of the college and its work. Although the rejection resulted from a number of handicaps under which the college labored, the impression went out, according to Dr. Haught, that the college was making athletics the goat. To set the record straight he read into the minutes of the Board of Trustees a letter from President Hughes which indicated that he had recommended that the college be accredited for one year to be reinspected in 1927. "Serious exception was taken to the athletic situation and the College was turned down on that ground, and I believe on that ground only. I strongly recommend that you take up this matter very carefully, and when this one matter is straightened up in a satisfactory way, I feel that there is no question but what West Virginia Wesleyan College will be accredited one year hence." Dean Haught recommended that the trustees evaluate the present athletic policy in the light of this development.

The problem with regard to athletics, which was not to be settled finally for a number of years, is difficult to determine since no records are available as to the precise nature of the accrediting agency's objections. The crux of the situation appears to have been that athletes at Wesleyan who made the varsity squad were being awarded tuition, room and board. They were housed and fed in the gymnasium. The issue was

61

not that the athletic program continued to run deficits. The gate receipt guarantees which Wesleyan received from the large schools with which it competed during the late twenties sometimes meant the difference between the budget of the college being weighted on the credit rather than the debit side of the ledger. Checks of considerable amounts which Coach "Cebe" Ross turned over to the college not infrequently provided the funds needed to meet the payroll. The objection of the North Central Association appears to have been that the assistance given to athletes amounted to a system of professional athletics.

During the year three fraternities and two sororities were organized following action by the Board of Trustees in the spring of 1925 permitting such organizations. This development proceeded under the supervision of a committee created by the trustees consisting of the president of the board, the president of the college and three members of the faculty. Of more than passing interest is the fact that the organization of fraternities and sororities was almost synonymous with the demise, for all practical purposes, of the Chrestomathean and Excelsior Literary Societies. Professor William Seifrit in his careful study of the rise and decline of these organizations at Wesleyan notes that they began to lose ground around 1911. With the steady growth of the student body beginning in 1910, it became increasingly difficult for the societies to function as they had been accustomed in their heyday in the face of student desire for more specialized activity, the growing emphasis on athletics, the rise of inter-collegiate debating, the coming of greater social freedom, and finally the inauguration of fraternities and sororities. The weekly debates in the societies gradually died out and were replaced by programs of music, singing, and humorous readings. Both societies began presenting music and variety shows. By 1915 formidable opposition came from two rival debating groups on campus, the Wesleyan Debating Club and the Webster Debating Club. Then came the Wesleyan Forensic Association under the direction of Professor Loren Staats. By 1928 this group had secured a local chapter of Pi Kappa Delta, a national forensic honorary. Dramatic Arts were dominated by The Wesleyan Players which came into existence during the twenties. By 1929-30, debating, drama and related media were under the speech department. By 1927 more than twenty-five student organizations had preempted the role of the Chrestomathean and Excelsior societies. A merger of the two groups that year failed to solve the problem of declining interest and attendance, and in 1937 they were no longer listed among the organizations on campus.

Dean Haught concerned himself also with what he referred to as the "attendance problem" and the need for increase in the revenues of the college. His report to the trustees noted that during the year sixty-six selected students had been sent to high schools throughout the state to try to create interest in Wesleyan. On the problem of finances he recommended that the trustees begin at once a campaign for $500,000 to increase the endowment, build a library, and care for a current expense deficit of $20,000. If such an amount could be raised to be paid in four or five annual payments enough money could be realized to secure the balance of $50,000 pledged to the college by the General Education Board. The campaign did not materialize.

The Board of Trustees meeting on June 7, 1926, elected to the presidency of the college, Dr. Homer E. Wark, professor of History of Religion at Boston University. Dr. Wark came to Wesleyan soon after his election. Among the concerns to which he gave priority was the problem of accreditation by the North Central Association of Colleges. He indicated that several problems stood in the way of accreditation according to the report of the review board. The college was enrolling too many special students. The teaching load for several members of the faculty was too large. The library was understaffed, facilities were limited, hours were inadequate, and there was no appropriation for books. In addition there was the problem of athletics.

In June 1926, following Dean Haught's suggestion, the trustees had taken action which revoked all authorization to assist athletes whether by "scholarships, rooms, or other financial support, either directly or indirectly" with the exception of those financed by endowments for this purpose. Dr. Wark noted, however, that against his advice the training table had continued. A letter from Dr. Hughes had indicated that this could hinder accreditation.

Pursuant to Dr. Wark's recommendation action was taken abolishing the training table, placing participation in athletics on a voluntary basis and endorsing the expansion of the intramural sports program. The trustees also constituted an Athletic Board which implemented the action taken.

During 1926-27 measures were adopted to remove the objections of the North Central Association of Colleges to the status of the library and to increase the facilities and use of the library. These actions included arrangements to keep the library open in the evening, the appropriation of $2,000 to be renewed on a yearly basis for enlarging and equipping the library, a recommendation that the next financial campaign include funds for the erection of a library building. The Board of Trustees also created a standing Library Committee.

During the first semester of 1927, the college again applied for admission to the North Central Association of Colleges, and at the June meeting of the trustees Dr. Wark announced that the school had been admitted to the association. Four years later in April 1931, the Association of University Women also admitted the school to membership.

The rising cost of operating the college, the growing competition among the colleges of the state for students, the annual deficits which plagued the college prompted Dr. Wark to recommend at the June 1927, meeting of the Board of Trustees a financial campaign for increasing the endowment, for the erection of new buildings and the retirement of the college's indebtedness. The most pressing needs in a building program included an extension to Agnes Howard Hall, a library and a dormitory for boys. The trustees approved Dr. Wark's suggestion and entered into a joint effort with the Wesley Foundation of West Virginia University. The goal was $500,000 and the receipts were to be shared on the basis of 80 per cent for Wesleyan College and 20 per cent for the Foundation. The joint effort resulted in the securing of $182,389 after expenses for the campaign in the amount of $25,116.88. A total of $44,000 was added to the endowment fund.

During 1927 the trustees authorized purchase of the Forman Hospital on Florida Street for $20,000 for use as a freshman boys' dormitory. It was purchased for $17,000 cash. It has been used variously as a dormitory, a boarding hall and a fraternity house. During 1928 the Board of Trustees authorized the construction of an addition to Agnes Howard Hall along with the repair of the old building and the equipping and furnishing of the whole, the project to be financed by a bond issue not to exceed $100,000. The issue was sold to the State of West Virginia for the School Fund Investment. The work was completed in time for occupancy the second semester of 1928-29 by the John W. Kisner and Brothers Lumber Company at a cost of $97,976.29.

The installation of an organ in Atkinson Hall was authorized by the trustees on June 3, 1930.

A number of items involving the academic life of the school received attention during Dr. Wark's administration. Freshman Week was observed for the first time in the autumn of 1929 with freshman students arriving five days before upperclassmen for orientation in college life. The trustees approved a change in the school week from a Tuesday to Saturday, to a Monday to Saturday noon schedule in order to bring Wesleyan in line with other state schools, to prevent a loss of classes by the debate and football teams which were often away on weekends and to keep Saturday free for extension courses. A special discount allowed to children of faculty members, ministers and ministerial students was discontinued. In lieu of the discount the trustees made available ten scholarships of one semester each, in addition to other scholarships which might be available, for deserving students who would otherwise be unable to attend college.

Social life at the college demanded attention at a number of points. Dr. Wark informed the Board of Trustees that the issues of dancing, drinking and gambling called for a more explicit policy by the board on these problems. College students were being allowed to attend dances off campus, but the college could not control the character of the dance halls. Faculty members objected to acting as chaperones. A special committee of the Board on Social and Religious Life made a survey of faculty, students, alumni and ministers which indicated strong sentiment for permitting dancing on campus under faculty supervision. However, in view of the strong stand taken against dancing by the General Conference and the 1928 Discipline of the Methodist Church, the committee recommended that the college retain its disapproval of dancing and in no case sponsor dances on or off campus. Parents wishing their children to dance while at Wesleyan were required to indicate this in writing to the dean. The faculty was charged with determining the frequency with which such students would be allowed to exercise the privilege. The faculty committee on social life was urged to work with the director of physical education and recreation in working out an adequate program of social activities for the school.

The recollection of one member of the Social Life Committee, who is still teaching at Wesleyan, is that during the late twenties the committee planned parties and other social events at which dancing was permitted. From this point, dances sponsored by college groups gradually became a part of the social life of the school, a development which coincided with a change in attitude on the part of the church itself toward dancing.

In 1929 the Board of Trustees gave permission to fraternities to purchase property with the understanding that the college would incur no financial or moral obligation either to pay for or to see that the property was paid for.

In 1930 under the sponsorship of President and Mrs. Wark an organization of the Student Volunteer Movement was founded. This organization evidently supplanted "The Wesleyan Volunteer Band" which came into existence prior to 1910 and was active for approximately eighteen years. The student volunteer group, like its predecessor, was primarily interested in the world missionary enterprise of the Christian church and in recruiting and bringing together those who would enter the field of foreign missions. However, it also sent gospel teams to churches in the vicinity of the college and with financial assistance from First Church, Buckhannon, opened a church school and prepared the ground for other areas of religious work in that section of Buckhannon known as the Liggett Addition.

Dr. Wark tendered his resignation as president of Wesleyan at the meeting of the Board of Trustees, July 7, 1930. He listed in his resignation a few items which he felt worthy of mention as indicating that a measure of progress had been made during his administration, namely, the settlement of athletic affairs in such a way as to save money and to make possible higher standards, the attainment of membership in the North Central Association of Colleges, the enlargement of Agnes Howard Hall and the acquisition of the boys' dormitory, the raising of about $93,000 on endowment and $67,000 on current indebtedness.

The Board of Trustees expressed its continued confidence in the work of Dr. Wark and declined to accept his resignation.

At the same meeting a special survey committee reported to the Board of Trustees its findings regarding the present status and future prospects of the college. The perennial problem of the school, the need for more money, received the bulk of the committee's attention. The report noted that over the past six years the income of the college had increased by 27.2 per cent while expenses had increased by 37.7 per cent. Immediate steps had to be taken to increase the endowment funds of the college and to find one hundred more students. The committee also registered its opinion that there were too many departments in the college, and that they should be reduced from fourteen to seven or eight. This would result in a saving to the college since under the present setup every professor was the head of a department. Dr. Wark suggested that the president's salary be cut $1,000 per year.

Dr. Wark tendered his resignation again in June 1931. In so doing he pointed out that West Virginia Wesleyan was now in the unique position of being on the accredited list of top agencies. It could appeal to "well-to-do" Methodists of the state to send their children to Wesleyan where they could get a first-rate education rather than sending them elsewhere. On the question of what kind of college Wesleyan ought to be, he suggested that it ought to concentrate on being an institution which could produce "broadly and culturally trained individuals." He urged leaving vocational training to the state. He felt that Wesleyan, and colleges like it, were being pressured to do too many things, to cover many practical fields, to train professionally and vocationally, and to do this superficially. Wesleyan might have to compromise the ideal for a time, but in the long run it should become the best cultural college in the state. For the present he suggested that the primary problem of the college was how to retain excellent teachers. There was undoubtedly a relationship between faculty turnover from year to year and the fact that the school had to pay some of its personnel pitiably small salaries.

The Board of Trustees accepted Dr. Wark's resignation and on July 1, 1931, unanimously elected to the office of president the Reverend Dr. Roy J. McCuskey, a member of the West Virginia Annual Conference.

Roy J. McCuskey was born June 19, 1883, in the Big Run Community near the town of Cameron in Marshall County, West Virginia. In November 1901, he enrolled in the West Virginia Conference Seminary and graduated with the class of 1905. In the fall of 1905 he was admitted to the West Virginia Conference of the Methodist Episcopal Church and assigned to the Cameron Circuit. The following year he returned to Wesleyan and served as pastor of the Holly Grove Circuit until 1908 when he completed the work for the Bachelor of Arts degree. The same fall he enrolled as a student in the Boston University School of Theology. While in school he served as pastor of the Methodist Church in Hingham, Massachusetts. In 1911 he received the degree of Bachelor of Sacred Theology and returned to West Virginia where he was admitted into full connection to the annual conference of the Methodist Episcopal Church. From 1911 until he was elected to the presidency of West

Virginia Wesleyan College in 1931, he served as pastor of Shinnston; North Street, Wheeling; Seventh Avenue, Huntington; St. Andrews, Parkersburg; and Thomson, Wheeling. He served as district superintendent of the Parkersburg District from 1920-26. He was a delegate to the General Conference of the Methodist Episcopal Church in 1924, 1932 and 1936, and to the General Conference of The Methodist Church in 1940. He was a member of the board of the Epworth League and of the University Senate of the Methodist Episcopal Church. In the West Virginia Conference he helped organize the Epworth League Institute and for several years worked in it and taught classes; served on the Board of Ministerial Training and taught in the Area School for Ministers; and was a member of the Conference Commission on World Service and Finance. From 1921 to 1941 he was a trustee of West Virginia Wesleyan College and was awarded the honorary degree of Doctor of Divinity by the college in 1922.

The work of Dr. McCuskey's administration was cut out for him even before he assumed leadership of the college. For the next ten years he would struggle with the problem of keeping the college from foundering on the rocks of financial disaster. The nation was in the midst of the industrial depression, the effect of which had been gradually worsening the financial situation of the college. During his first two years as president, Dr. McCuskey had to report decreases in investments, decreases in apportionments from the annual conference Board of Education, loss of money in various departments of the school. The closing of the banks in Buckhannon had tied up $6,000 of current expense money, making it necessary to borrow money to meet the monthly payroll and other bills. Banks from which the college had the heaviest loans were asking for payments or more collateral. The college was meeting deficits by selling securities from the endowment fund, by using money which had been pledged on endowment gifts, or by using capital funds for current budget. As of 1932 the college was in debt on loans in the amount of $110,000 plus the bonds of $91,000 outstanding on Agnes Howard Hall.

To add to the woes of the college the North Central Association dropped Wesleyan from its list of accredited institutions. In discussing this development in his autobiography, Dr. McCuskey reports that among the reasons for the loss of accreditation was the objection of the association to the loans and other financial assistance being awarded to athletes. As attempt had been made to deal with what was referred to as the "athletic problem" by the establishment of the Wesleyan Student Loan Board, Inc., by the Alumni Athletic Board. The administration of aid to athletes, despite the adjustments which had been made during Dr. Wark's presidency, continued to be the severest point of criticism. Much of the money in the loan fund came from alumni donations. Theoretically, loans were to be made to any student at Wesleyan on the basis of individual need. However, in practice, most of the loans were made to athletes. Some loans were repaid, but some recipients apparently did not understand that they were loans and did not believe that it was necessary to repay them. Since part of the loan fund could be traced from athletic profits through the fund to the athletes, they were interpreted as gifts when they were not repaid. The administration did not feel that it could accede to the request of the North Central Association that the college discontinue all loans at once, since this course of action would have been unjust to those already enrolled and engaged in an honest effort to complete their education. Dr. McCuskey believed that the association could have been more generous in its treatment of Wesleyan on this matter, inasmuch as the amount Wesleyan and other small colleges were putting into athletics was a pittance compared to huge amounts being expended by larger colleges and universities where accreditation was continued by the association.

Early in Dr. McCuskey's administration, however, the loan fund was discontinued. For approximately ten years during the McCuskey administration athletes earned room and board serving as janitors, raking leaves and doing whatever odd jobs the college was able to give them.

A satisfactory solution to the problem of aid to athletes was slow in coming, and perhaps this is a logical point to indicate the outcome. During World War II intercollegiate athletic competition was discontinued. Following the war the majority of athletes attended school under the program of government assistance for veterans, and financial aid for athletes was not a problem. When the flow of veterans trickled to a halt, a number of grants-in-aid were made available to athletes. The number of such grants eventually added up to thirteen worth $200 each. In 1951 Wesleyan dropped football as an intercollegiate sport, but continued basketball. Football was resumed in the fall of 1953, in part, because of difficulty in recruiting students who wanted to attend school where there was no football team. Interestingly, most of the pressure came from prospective women students. The venture back into intercollegiate competition was designated "educational football," a term which means that the football teams were composed of regularly enrolled students who wanted to play football. In the absence of any incentive for top rated football material to attend Wesleyan, the fortunes of the football teams were at low ebb for a period of about five years. During the early years of the present administration a system of Merit Awards was established, distributed among all the departments of the college. Ten of these awards were allocated for basketball and thirty for football. This aid was a boon to the athletic program. The same number of awards are allocated to the athletic department as of this writing, though the amount of each award has been increased from $400 to $500 per year as tuition has risen. The aim had been to place Wesleyan in a competitive position with many of the state schools with which the Wesleyan teams must play. However, the amount of the awards has not kept pace with rising costs. Athletes who receive the awards must be recommended by the coach, and the awards are approved in the same manner as any other scholarship. To keep the award a student must maintain a C average and must not be subject to any disciplinary action. Further, an athlete who receives a Merit Award does so with the understanding that it is a partial workship in the Department of Physical Education.

The loss of accreditation by the North Central Association was not due solely to the difficulty involving athletics. According to Dr. McCuskey, Wesleyan would have lost its accreditation even if the school had fully complied with the demand that the loans to athletes be discontinued. The North Central Association had suggested that faculty standards were low. The financial posture also affected the standing of the college. However, Dr. McCuskey suggested that the board should not deal "in too drastic fashion" with salaries inasmuch as faculty members were already returning uncomplainingly 5 per cent of their salary to the budget. It was hardly fair to ask the employees of the college to bear all the burden of balancing the budget.

Measures were adopted to meet the emergency. The trustees in May 1932, authorized the issuing of $100,000 worth of 6 per cent fifteen year Gold Bonds to become due and payable April 1, 1947. In May of 1932, the salaries of employees and faculty were reduced by 25 per cent from an average of $2,433 to an average of $1,812. No catalogue was issued for 1933-34. The West Virginia Annual Conference was asked to support the college at the rate of 50 cents per member plus designated gifts.

70

Still the crisis deepened. Early in 1933, Dr. McCuskey reported the loss of most of the endowment securities of the college. It could secure no long-term loans. Faculty members, long patient under trying circumstances and all of whom were in debt to Buckhannon merchants, were beginning to wonder whether they would ever receive all that the college had promised them. In addition, the school was faced with combatting two issues which had been making the rounds for some time. First, there were those who were saying that the church college was an archaic institution, that there were too many church colleges, particularly in the Methodist Church. The younger and weaker should be permitted to die and efforts should be devoted to saving the big institutions. Second, a rumor, purportedly emanating from Wesleyan itself, had been broadcast to the effect that it would be impossible to continue the institution. Dr. McCuskey affirmed his belief that the school could remain, that it ought to remain. Methodists of the state should sacrifice to keep it going, else they did not deserve the name Methodist!

Evidence of the determination to keep Wesleyan alive came out of the meeting of the Board of Trustees in the autumn of 1933. First, the office of vice president was created with the Reverend Mr. John E. Hanifan, a member of the West Virginia Annual Conference, being elected to the office. The specific duties of the vice president were to solicit students, and to direct a financial campaign. Second, plans were announced for a special day at the college on October 5, to be known as "Bishop's Day." The attempt would be made to secure the attendance of a large number of members of the annual conference, laymen and friends. The bishop of the West Virginia Annual Conference would be the guest of honor and would deliver an address. Third, a resolution was adopted and sent to each pastor and lay delegate of the annual conference urging collection of the annual apportionment on each charge of 50 cents per member for the support of Wesleyan.

By June 1934, $60,000 worth of the Gold Bonds issued two years earlier had been sold. While the money gained had not reduced the indebtedness of the college, which was now over a quarter of a million dollars, it had reduced a large proportion of what was owed to merchants and faculty. Indebtedness to the faculty was reduced by $20,266.43 though it was noted that the faculty itself had subscribed for bonds in the amount of $16,500.

Midway through President McCuskey's tenure a turning point was reached in the struggle of Wesleyan to survive. The year 1934-35 showed a definite brightening of the school's prospects. Dr. McCuskey reported to the Board of Trustees in June 1935, that enrollment showed a 27 per cent increase over the previous year. Income from students had risen. The churches had begun to respond with greater financial assistance. The market value of endowment securities had advanced and some back interest had been paid. The college had been approved by the University Senate, the standardizing body of the Methodist Episcopal Church. Dean Oscar Lambert reported that a committee appointed to determine the eligibility of the school for reaccreditation by the North Central Association had reported a hopeful estimate.

Dr. McCuskey turned his attention to the future and suggested a number of objectives for the school. Foremost among these was the re-gaining of accreditation by the North Central Association. The meeting of standards required by the association would involve adjustments in the area of faculty, curriculum, salaries, endowment, control of athletics. The president proposed a study of the steps necessary to meet require-ments of the association, but he cautioned against hasty action which might involve the embarrassment of another retreat. Of equal importance was the strengthening of the financial standing of the college. The en-dowment would have to be rebuilt to pre-depression status plus an additional half-million dollars. Support from constituency, churches and alumni would have to be increased. The indebtedness must be paid. Attention needed to be given to increasing the enrollment to 550 or 600 full-time students. In this connection Dr. McCuskey noted that the Executive Committee was contemplating a special effort to reach stu-dents in the metropolitan area of New York and certain sections of New Jersey and Pennsylvania. The lower tuition rate at Wesleyan was attractive to out-of-state students of moderate circumstances. Finally, Dr. McCuskey suggested that plans should be made to celebrate the approach-ing Fiftieth Anniversary of the college. The celebration should cover a two-year period, 1938-40, and should include a development program which would provide for the payment of all indebtedness, put all build-ings into good repair, raise an additional endowment of at least $500,000 and provide for a much needed library building.

A committee appointed to plan the semi-centennial celebration pro-duced a comprehensive program:

1. The preparation of a history of the college to be off the press before the June commencement of 1940.
2. The preparation of a pageant for the occasion of the fiftieth anniversary.
3. Visitation of the churches of the conference by the president, the vice president and other representatives of the college.
4. The offering of suitable prizes to winners of a contest in the production of a new Wesleyan College song or songs.
5. A careful survey of the buildings and grounds of the college by competent architects and landscape artists so that any anticipated changes in buildings or relocation of any facilities would be done in a way which would conserve the beauty of the campus.
6. The drawing of plans for a library building and the attempt to find a way of financing the structure.
7. The planning of a major financial campaign which would liquidate all debts; add the greatest possible sum to the endowment, including special projects such as professorships and scholarships; provide for the building of a library and a heating plant; put all buildings in good repair and improve the grounds.

The committee suggested that the financial campaign should begin at the commencement of 1938, and that the program of celebration should begin with the commencement of 1940 and continue through the meeting of the annual conference with the conference being invited to meet at Buckhannon.

Dr. Wallace B. Fleming, after fifteen years as president of Baker University, Baldwin, Kansas, returned to Wesleyan in 1937 as vice president to organize and direct the Semi-Centennial Campaign. The goal for the campaign was $1,000,000. Of this amount $250,000 was to be used for debt retirement, $25,000 for property improvement and repairs; $200,000 for a library and endowment of same, $500,000 for the endowment, and $25,000 for expenses of the semi-centennial celebration.

The campaign was launched at a rally in First Methodist Church, Clarksburg, March 26, 1939. The occasion brought together all except one of the living former presidents. Dr. Carl G. Doney was the speaker. Subsequent rallies were held in each of the districts of the conference by the end of June.

The results of the campaign fell far short of the goal. As of May 31, 1940, the total in cash and pledges was $489,540. An emergency appeal brought in enough to run the total safely above the half million mark by the time of commencement. Dr. Fleming noted that the effort had proceeded under difficult circumstances resulting from the economic depression including shutdowns in the coal industry, general unemployment and the fear of people to commit themselves for more than a year.

A major bequest to the college came in 1937. Calvin A. West, a native West Virginian, by the terms of his will provided that the income from his estate should go to certain relatives while they lived. When specific bequests were cared for, the balance of the estate should be transferred to Wesleyan as part of the permanent endowment fund to be used for scholarships and to be known as "The Calvin A. West Scholarship Fund." It was estimated that the estate would amount to approximately $200,000.

The Semi-Centennial Planning Committee concluded that some progress had been made on all objectives of the financial campaign except the erection of a library building. The problem of application for readmission to membership in the North Central Association successively postponed through the thirties because of fear that the standards of the college were not up to the demands of that agency remained unsolved. This situation resulted in loss of membership in the American Association of University Women. Dr. McCuskey pointed out also that the rating of the school with the University Senate was none too high.

The year of the fiftieth anniversary was observed by a variety of events on campus. Dr. Frank B. Trotter was the speaker for the first convocation, September 22, 1939. Bishop's Day was observed October 27. The annual homecoming was held October 28. Handel's *Messiah* was presented before the Christmas recess. Religious Emphasis Week was observed February 12-18, 1940, with Dr. Frank T. Cartwright, Associate Secretary of the Board of Foreign Missions of the former Methodist Episcopal Church, as speaker. The West Virginia Conference Intercollegiate Basketball Tournament and the West Virginia Intercollegiate Speech Festival were held on campus in March. April 15-19 was observed as "Good Government Week," a program initiated by Dr. McCuskey in 1937, aimed at developing honest and good citizens. Commencement week, June 2-5, included a conference on college education conducted by Dr. Guy Snavely, Executive Director of the Association of American Colleges; the presentation of a pageant of West Virginia Wesleyan College written by Miss Jean Latham, a graduate of the class of 1925; and a commencement address by Bishop Adna Wright Leonard of the Methodist Episcopal Church.

Despite the adverse circumstances under which the college operated during the decade of the thirties, the mood and tone of the college was neither one of pessimism nor of simply holding the line. Varied and significant developments took place in a number of areas over the period from 1931-40.

Under the leadership of Dean Oscar D. Lambert a summer school extension course was established in Logan directed by Dr. Thomas Haught. A summer music camp of eight weeks for high school students was inaugurated. The divisional organization of the college was revamped in 1934 under five divisions. The Business Department which had been eliminated as part of the retrenchment of the college program early in the thirties was restored as a result of popular demand for courses in the field.

Distinguished lecturers were brought to the campus under the influence of the Dean of Women, Mrs. C. Edmond Neal. These included Dr. F. K. Morris who lectured on his role in the exposition which found dinosaur eggs in the Gobi Desert, and Robert Frost who read from his own poems.

The library facilities were expanded and the collection was increased to twenty thousand volumes. The Library Committee of the Board of Trustees, with Mr. Phil Conley as chairman, sponsored an annual Library Day to stimulate the giving of books and funds to the library.

Dr. George Glauner coached a number of successful debating teams, and in 1934 Wesleyan was the only college in the state to have representation in the Pi Kappa Alpha National Debating Tournament.

In 1937 a committee of the Board of Trustees presented a resolution establishing a retirement plan in the form of a deferred annuity contract issued by the Teacher's Insurance and Annuity Association with the college and the participant each contributing 5 per cent of the participant's salary. Participation was made mandatory after two years' service. The age of retirement was set at sixty-five with provision made for employment by special vote of the trustees for extension of services for definite periods of time up to the end of the academic year in which the age seventy was reached. Final approval of the plan came in 1938.

The first issue of the Alumni Magazine was published during the school year 1936-37. First mention of the strawberry festival to be held on campus appeared in the minutes of the Board of Trustees for June 1937.

The year 1939 was a momentous one for Methodism in view of the uniting of the three major Methodist bodies into one church. Early discussion of the implications of this event indicated that the leaders of the college hoped that Wesleyan might become the one really outstanding liberal arts college in the state. The question facing West Virginia Methodism and the church at large was whether or not it could support two institutions. The first fifty years of Wesleyan came to a close with her future unsettled.

IV

THE BEGINNINGS OF GROWTH

Dr. McCuskey resigned as president of Wesleyan at the June 1941 meeting of the Board of Trustees. He had suggested a year previous that consideration be given his successor. The board accepted his decision and appointed Dr. Wallace Fleming as acting president.

On July 31, 1941, the *Republican Delta,* local Buckhannon weekly newspaper, published a special issue dedicated to West Virginia Wesleyan College and to Dr. Roy McCuskey on the occasion of his retirement. In a lead article headlined "What Kind of College is West Virginia Wesleyan?" Dr. McCuskey affirmed that Wesleyan was fulfilling its role as a Christian college under Methodist control. Of the 61 colleges of The Methodist Church, Wesleyan now stood tenth in the number of Methodist students enrolled, 61 per cent, with only 3.5 per cent of the student body having no church preference. Full-time enrollment hovered around the 450 mark with the values of the small college class, personal contacts and supervision of student activities and work, being retained. For the future an expansion of enrollment to 650 or 700 would match reasonably the normal growth of the student population of the state. Such expansion would require addition to all facilities and personnel. The Board of Trustees had received preliminary studies of the campus for placement of buildings which should come eventually—library, music and fine arts building, chapel, dormitory for men, a student center, and some changes in athletic facilities.

However, he added, unless some fairy in the form of a very wealthy man or women should appear suddenly, Wesleyan would have to follow the slow process of gathering friends in order not only to hold present ground but to advance.

William D. Foster, in "What Wesleyan Means to Buckhannon," noted that the college was the outstanding human enterprise in the community. In the past year the college had expended $151,415 in salaries, plant, equipment and maintenance costs. Students at Wesleyan spent $150,000 in Buckhannon. If the 127 students from Buckhannon enrolled at Wesleyan had left the community to attend school elsewhere

77

they would have taken more than $60,000 yearly with them from the community. Without Wesleyan many local boys and girls would be unable to attend college for financial reasons.

The annual session of the West Virginia Conference meeting in June 1940 had granted Wesleyan the privilege of continuing its Semi-Centennial Campaign. At the same time it requested the General Board of Education of The Methodist Church to make a study of the needs of the conference concerning educational institutions and to recommend what the conference program should be with respect to its two colleges— West Virginia Wesleyan and Morris Harvey, the college of the former Methodist Episcopal Church South.

Bishop James H. Straughn informed the trustees in June 1941, that the General Conference had authorized a committee to study the situation. The committee consisted of H. J. Burgstahler, president of Ohio Wesleyan College, as chairman; John Seaton, president of Albion College; Umphrey Lee, president of Southern Methodist University, and J. Earl Moreland, president of Randolph-Macon College. The findings of this committee led to action in the 1941 session of the West Virginia Annual Conference permitting Morris Harvey College to withdraw from The Methodist Church. Thereby the conference relinquished all interest in Morris Harvey leaving the college to be used and operated as the trustees of the institution should desire. In turn, Morris Harvey relinquished all financial claim for support or maintenance from the West Virginia Conference. West Virginia Wesleyan was now the sole college in the state owned and operated by The Methodist Church.

Early in 1942 the Board of Trustees adopted the report of a joint committee of the trustees and the members of the Board of Education of the Annual Conference aimed at coordinating the work of the college and the conference. The District Superintendent and the Executive Secretary of the Board of Education were made ex-officio members of the Board of Trustees upon election to office. The Conference Board of Education was given headquarters at the college without rent. Provision was made for college cooperation in developing the total educational program of the annual conference.

Concurrently, plans were being made for application for readmission to membership in the North Central Association. Dean Lambert attended the meeting of the Minnesota North Central Association during the summer of 1941. He noted that he had counseled with informed persons, visited campuses of member colleges, prepared standards and returned with the conviction that Wesleyan, by assuming special burdens, would be able to reach North Central Association standards. Following application for readmission during the interim presidency of Dr. Wallace Fleming, an inspection team from the North Central Association visited the campus during February 1942. The committee, consisting of President Gage of Lindenwood College, Dean Hyde of Mount Union College and Mr. MacKenzie of the University of Chicago, approved the college for a conditional two-year membership. Dean Lambert reported that the profile of the college worked out by the North Central Association inspection team noted that the weakness of the college included financial instability; a record of bad practice in financial administration; poor care of buildings; inadequate facilities for the library, and the Art and Home Economics Departments; too small instructional staff in relation to number of students; a disproportionate number of athletes receiving some form of financial aid; inadequate training of library staff; no organized student placement service; little opportunity for student representation in the faculty committees.

Among the strong points of the college were the retirement plan; the arrangements which held the promise of financial support from The Methodist Church; productive scholarship of the faculty; unusually strong work in chemistry and biology; strong work in English and teacher education; the high degree of faculty education; the record of graduates in post-graduate work; the high degree of success of alumni; the women's dormitory, the size of campus and arrangement of buildings; and the representation of denominational clientele in the student body. The faculty and administration constituted the strongest feature of the college. With some pressure coming from the North Central Association, Dean Lambert reported that the curriculum had been regrouped into four divisions: Natural Science; Social Science; Psychology, Education and Religion; Languages, Literature and Fine Arts. The foreign language requirement for graduation had been dropped due to the conviction that Wesleyan was losing potential students to institutions which had no language requirement, and that the requirement was an archaic holdover from the European educational system. Growing out of the North Central Association report two items were recommended to the Board of Trustees for study, a plan of leave of absence for teachers, and a ranking of faculty in the light of the standards and recommendations of the North Central Association. On February 11, 1943, the board approved the ranking of faculty in keeping with the standards of the North Central Association Committee—professors, associate professors, assistant professors and instructors. The policy of the American Association of University Professors on academic tenure was adopted. It was not until October 20, 1956, however, that a plan of sabbatical leaves for faculty was put into effect.

In 1944 Dr. Arthur A. Schoolcraft was elected Dean of Wesleyan.

Dr. Schoolcraft (1897-1959) was born in Euclid, West Virginia. After completing his undergraduate work at Marietta College, he attended Boston University where he earned the degrees of Bachelor of Sacred Theology and the Doctor of Philosophy. He subsequently studied at Harvard and at the University of Berlin. He came to Wesleyan in 1932 to teach in the Department of Education. He was dean of the college from 1944 until his death in 1959. He also held the position of registrar for most of these years. On two occasions, 1945 and 1956, he assumed the added responsibility of acting president of the college.

As dean, his impact on the college is best attested to by the estimate of his colleagues on the faculty. On the occasion of his death in 1959, a memorial by the faculty affirmed:

> The dean was a remarkable person who was ambitious, never for himself, only for his college. Like all successful men, he had a goal, that of guiding Wesleyan to a position of distinction among the colleges of the world.
>
> Because he was so alert and well informed, he was able to sustain the college during periods of financial stress and low enrollment, to gain accreditation for it as well as grants from many sources, to improve the caliber of personnel in all areas.
>
> His achievements exacted a staggering amount of application. The fact that he did more work than could be expected of one man, and the story of the unfailing light from his office windows every night (weekends, vacations, and holidays included) have become legends. All that he produced was meticulously well done. Even routine reports, which might elicit no more than an impatient glance before being consigned to the nearest wastebasket, were done with unusual care and polish.
>
> No matter how busy he was, he always had time for the problems of others. He considered nothing trivial that concerned the welfare of the college. He tempered his concern with wit and was always able to convey perspective to the issue at hand.
>
> The dean loved people. It was through his love for humanity that he set about removing the bars of prejudice and caused numbers of students from other nations and races to come to Wesleyan.
>
> Arthur Allen Schoolcraft laid a solid foundation on which a larger and greater

future may be built. To paraphrase Lincoln's Gettysburg Address, "the world will little note nor long remember what we say here, but it will never forget what he did here."

During his tenure as dean, Dr. Schoolcraft worked hard at raising the standards at Wesleyan so that the school could qualify for membership in other recognized accrediting agencies. Accreditation by the North Central Association opened the way for recognition by these agencies but progress was slow. Membership in the American Council on Education was announced in 1946, accreditation by the University Senate of New York in 1947, and by the University Senate of The Methodist Church in 1948. Wesleyan was readmitted to membership by the American Association of University Women in 1954 after the school took steps to meet the objection of the association to the dearth of women on the faculty and staff. Associate membership in the National Association of Schools of Music came in 1957 following the appointment of a departmental head of the school of music, the strengthening of offerings in music education and the inauguration on June 1, 1951, of the degree of Bachelor of Music Education. Full membership and accreditation in NASM came subsequently in 1964.

The Board of Education reporting to the 1942 session of the annual conference noted the action of the North Central Association. The report of the committee of the General Conference was brought to the attention of the conference. The report noted that the building and grounds of the college had an estimated value of one-half million dollars. The productive endowment had been estimated at approximately $200,000 while the indebtedness was about $100,000. The report indicated that the school needed an increase in current income of from $50,000 to $100,000. An endowment of at least $400,000 was needed to raise salaries from the thirteenth percentile to a reasonable level of a seventy-fifth percentile in the North Central Area. The need for additional facilities would necessitate an outlay of at least $762,000. In sum, an aggregate of $1,447,000 would be required to meet these basic needs.

In the midst of these events a new president for Wesleyan was elected April 17, 1942, in the person of Dr. Joseph Warren Broyles. Born and reared in Eastern Tennessee, Dr. Broyles did his undergraduate work at Tusculum College, received the Bachelor's degree from the Boston University School of Theology and the Ph.D. degree from Drew University. He served three pastorates in the Holston Conference of the Methodist

Episcopal Church South, and taught at Hamline University. Prior to his election to the presidency of Wesleyan he was president of Snead Junior College at Boaz, Alabama.

Dr. Fleming once again assumed the office of vice-president. The Board of Trustees in a fitting tribute took notice of the distinguished service he had rendered Wesleyan and of the substantial role he had played in getting the school restored to membership in the North Central Association. During his first term as president Dr. Fleming composed Wesleyan's alma mater song. In 1944 he resigned as vice-president sixty days previous to his seventy-second birthday.

Before Dr. Broyles' election, Acting President Fleming had suggested to the Board of Trustees that while the report of the Commission of the General Board of Education was fresh in the memory of the annual conference a plea should be made for a campaign to increase the financial resources of the college by an amount sufficient to undergird the work the college ought to do. Accordingly, Dr. Broyles presented to the annual conference of 1942 a Program of Advance for West Virginia Wesleyan College. The annual conference approved the program and the raising of funds necessary to implement it, to be completed between January 1, 1943, and January 1, 1944, under the direction of the Conference Board of Education, the administration of the college, and the Bishop of the Pittsburgh Area.

Action was taken by the annual conference on another matter affecting the work of the college. The North Central Association report had ranked the college in the below-average percentile rating in the area of general control of the institution because of the large proportion of ministers on the Board of Trustees. Direct responsibility was not laid on the ministers for unwise business management, but it was suggested that the board ought to have a more adequate representation of business and professional men and women. The trustees petitioned the annual conference to gradually reduce the number of trustees from forty to twenty-four elective members plus three ex-officio members, and to provide for nomination of trustees by a committee rather than from the floor of the annual conference. It was suggested also that so far as was practical two-thirds of those elected should be laymen and one-third ministers, and that at least one woman and one alumnus of the college be among the lay persons elected each year. Terms of service were to run from one to four years. The annual conference voted to maintain a fifty-fifty representation of laymen and ministers. In order to retain experienced laymen, the Board of Trustees voted to continue the original board of forty members.

The year 1942 marked a turning point in the financial status of the college. In September Mr. Lawrence Lynch, a trustee, announced that Mrs. L. L. Loar had given the college real estate in Clarksburg at an agreed value of $17,000. Mr. A. F. McCue, a trustee, noted that this gift was the initial increment toward the total cost of a building at Wesleyan to be used as a music hall and dedicated to the memory of the L. L. Loar family. Mrs. Loar also had expressed her intention to provide at least $100,000 for that purpose.

The significant achievement of the year was the retirement of the indebtedness of the college. The efforts of Mr. Lawrence Lynch and Mr. Anthony McCue effected a settlement of the bond issue for the erection of the addition to Agnes Howard Hall purchased in 1928 and 1929 by the Board of the School Fund of the State of West Virginia at par and annual interest of $101,513. Over the years the college retired bonds and paid interest which had reduced the value of the bonds and interest due to $62,000. As of October 28, 1940, however, principle and interest due had risen to $142,539 due to default in payments. A conference with Governor Matthew M. Neely produced an agreement whereby the state would settle for a sum which, added to principal and interest already paid, would equal the original amount invested. On December 24, 1942, President Broyles and trustees L. L. Lynch, Anthony McCue and A. V. G. Upton delivered to Charleston a check for $40,893 and returned home with the bonds which had been there since 1928. Of this amount $36,500 in new money had been raised by the trustees over a period of a month. The balance came from payments on the Semi-Centennial Fund.

An equally important accomplishment was the settling of the Gold Bond issue of 1932. Interest of 6 per cent on the bonds was paid regularly and many bonds were turned into the college as payments on the Semi-Centennial Campaign pledges. By the middle of May 1942, only $33,000 of the bonds were outstanding. An attempt to refund these by the issuing of 3 per cent bonds resulted in the exchange of some old bonds for the new issue. Many were returned to the college outright, while some holders requested cash for their bonds and received it. By September the amount of bonds outstanding had been reduced to $10,400. The Board of Trustees then authorized the Empire National Bank of Clarksburg as trustee to call such bonds for redemption and payment on October 1, 1942. More bonds were turned in as gifts than were presented for cash so that by January 1943, the remaining bonds and isolated interest coupons had been reduced to $1,027. The college delivered to the bank an indemnifying bond in that amount securing the issue. The collateral security was delivered to the Union Trust Company of Pittsburgh. The remaining bonds were retired April 1944.

At the meeting of the Board of Trustees which passed the resolution retiring the Gold Bond issue, Mr. Anthony McCue presented the following summary of the college's stature which he entitled "Do You Know?":

Do You Know?

1. That the buildings of this institution are in the best state of repair they have been in for the past ten years.

2. That we have the best fire protection possible.

3. That the properties have been reappraised for insurance purposes and we have the lowest insurance rate in the history of the institution.

4. That when Mr. Lawrence Lynch's resolution with reference to retirement of bonds has been carried out, the College will be completely out of debt.

5. That the Treasurer of the College is doing a capital job.

6. That we are now discounting all bills for the first time in the history of the college.

7. That our department in Chemistry is head and shoulders above such department in any other school in the State of West Virginia including the State University. That the students from the Chemistry Department of West Virginia Wesleyan College have jobs the next day after graduation, if they want them.

8. That we have the best financial advice obtainable through the services of the Union Trust Company of Pittsburgh, a conservative, safe trust company.

9. That today we own more government bonds than the College ever dreamed it would have.

10. That The Methodist Church is giving greater support to the College than ever before in its history.

At this point the financial situation was such that a 12 per cent increase in salary was granted, but at the same time the rule granting free tuition to faculty children was repealed.

Dr. Broyles died suddenly on September 29, 1945. Arthur A. Schoolcraft was designated acting president, as well as dean of the college. He served in this capacity until the election to the office of president of Dr. William J. Scarborough on August 19, 1946.

The following year Dr. Schoolcraft recommended a further increase of 10 per cent in the salary scale in order to give the school a competitive advantage in securing much needed new personnel. The Board of Trustees adopted his recommendation. Dr. Schoolcraft also reported that prospects for students following a post World War II slump were "disconcertingly good," and the problem for several years ahead would be how to provide faculty and facilities for the anticipated student body. The acute housing shortage would be relieved somewhat by the assignment by the Federal Public Housing Authority of temporary dormitories for eighty veterans and twenty family units for married veterans to be ready for occupancy by September 1946. Wesleyan, he noted, had received also $10,000 worth of war surplus property for use in laboratories and shops for only the cost of crating and transportation.

Dr. William Scarborough came to Wesleyan from Morningside College, Sioux City, Iowa, where he had been dean of the college and professor of philosophy and religion since 1943. He was born in Lincoln, Nebraska. He received the A.B. degree from Hamline University in 1933, and from Boston University he received the M.A. degree in 1935, the S.T.B. degree in 1936, and the Ph.D. degree in 1940. During his college and university years he held pastorates. From 1939 to 1942 Dr. Scarborough was professor of philosophy and religion and dean of men at McKendree College, Lebanon, Illinois. During the year 1942-43 he was professor of psychology and religion and dean of the chapel at Cornell College, Mt. Vernon, Iowa. He was admitted to membership in the Minnesota Conference of the Methodist Episcopal Church in 1932, and subsequently held membership in the Southern Illinois Conference and the Upper Iowa Conference.

On the day of Dr. Scarborough's election as president in 1946, Mr. Anthony McCue announced that at the solicitation of Dr. Broyles, Mrs. Annie Merner Pfeiffer of New York had committed herself to a gift of $100,000 for a library building subject to two conditions: (1) funds were to be made available when construction of the building commenced, (2) at least two other buildings of equal cost were to be constructed at the same time. In her will Mrs. Pfeiffer also left a substantial amount of money to the Methodist General Board of Education for distribution at its discretion. Upon recommendation of Dr. John O. Gross, secretary of the board, Wesleyan was given subsequently an additional $50,000 for the library fund.

The bequest of Mrs. Lawson Loar was also finalized in 1946 with the provision in her will of $100,000 for the erection of the Loar Memorial Hall of Music and Fine Arts and an additional $150,000 endowment for the equipment and maintenance of the building.

In the summer of 1948 it was announced that Mrs. Calvin West, who had become a member of the Board of Trustees after her husband's death, had provided $100,000 in her will for the erection of a chapel to be known as the Calvin A. West Memorial Chapel.

Mr. L. C. Shingleton of Clarksburg, for many years a member of the Board of Trustees of the college, died in April 1948. His will provided that the entire residue of his estate, after providing a lifetime income for his widow, should become a part of the permanent endowment fund of West Virginia Wesleyan College.

In order to build the two structures required to claim the Pfeiffer gift, the Board of Trustees established at the suggestion of Judge Harry Shaw of Fairmont, a project called "The Boys' Dormitory Building Fund" which would attempt to find one hundred individuals who would contribute $1,000 each. During 1945-46 and concluding in 1947, under the direction of Dr. Fleming, the project secured $212,000.

Mr. Clyde O. Law, chairman of the Board of Trustees, proposed in 1947 that a series of objectives ought to be adopted to be achieved by 1950, the sixtieth anniversary of the school. These included the upgrading of the faculty and the social, intellectual and moral climate at Wesleyan; the attraction of intellectually capable and morally able students; the erection of six new buildings and provision for adequate equipment; the development of Christian youth leadership with the support and cooperation of the church. In short, Wesleyan ought to become a unique intellectual and spiritual center which would produce wholesome light and leadership for the two hundred thousand Methodist constituents in West Virginia.

Dr. Scarborough, in the same vein, noted that Wesleyan's total assets now stood at an all-time high of $1,180,000 including endowment, building fund and plant assets. He suggested serious consideration of a program including the erection of the proposed buildings, the increase of the college assets to at least two million dollars, a total student body of 850 and an annual operating budget of $500,000.

The chairman of the Building Committee of the Board of Trustees, Mr. Clinton F. Israel of Clarksburg, reported that the committee was of the opinion that the time had arrived for definite action on the location of new buildings on campus. According to present estimates it would require $700,000 to erect one wing of a men's dormitory, the library, the hall of music and fine arts, and a new heating plant.

Mr. Israel outlined the extensive steps taken in the development of the building program from 1945-47, including consultation with the architectural firm of Poundstone, Ayers and Godwin of Atlanta, Georgia; landscape architects Frank Harris, formerly landscape supervisor of the Greenbrier Hotel, now employed by Michael Benedum as supervisor of the Bridgeport Cemetery; and H. Boyer Marx, for a number of years Senior Site Planning Architect of the United States Housing Authority.

The Board of Trustees authorized adoption of the sites recommended for the men's dormitory, the library, the hall of music and fine arts, a maintenance building, and the production of draft drawings for two wings of the men's dormitory. These buildings are now located on the approximate sites recommended. However, objection was raised to location of the chapel between Agnes Howard Hall and the Administration Building. Bishop James Straughn counselled against placing the chapel "off on one side." It ought to be located at the dominant spot on the campus where it would symbolize the fact that Wesleyan is a Christian College and that everything about the institution is grouped around the centrality of the Christian faith. The chapel should be at the "very heart and center of the campus."

The Policy Commission of the board recommended a campaign to raise the money needed to qualify for the Pfeiffer gift, and requested the executors of the Annie Merner Pfeiffer Estate to transfer the money provided for the erection of the library to the General Board of Education in Nashville to be held in trust until the college could meet the conditions of the grant.

Impetus was given to the program of expansion by a resolution of the annual conference in September 1947, requesting the president and Board of Trustees of the college to investigate the possibility of using the college and its facilities as the site for sessions of the conference. A committee appointed to plan the sixtieth anniversary of the college explained the proposition. Recognizing that the dormitory space of the college would accommodate two hundred individuals, and assuming that the college shortly would have in hand money for the erection of one unit of the men's dormitory, the committee noted that before the college could entertain the annual conference several needs must be met: (1) an auditorium would have to be found with a seating capacity of twelve hundred, (2) a second unit of the boys' dormitory and a new women's dormitory would need to be erected, (3) the time of the annual conference and the sessions of the school would have to be integrated, (4) equipment and provisions for feeding the conference would have to be obtained. Acting on the study of the committee the Board of Trustees adopted a resolution petitioning the annual conference to adopt as a quadrennial project the raising of $750,000 to finance the needed expansion of the college and provide the facilities necessary to make the institution a permanent home for the annual conference. The college would attempt to raise another $1,250,000 from other sources for a total of $2,000,000. The program would be known as the West Virginia Wesleyan Capital Fund Campaign, would be the first item of concern for the quadrennium, and would be a ten-year venture.

At its annual meeting, the West Virginia Annual Conference took action which permitted the college to proceed with the campaign. It did not authorize a campaign of quota solicitation among the churches but urged ministers and congregations to give the effort their active support. It further recommended that the conference give first consideration to the college as soon as it seemed advisable to conduct a new fund-raising campaign.

Pursuant to the action of the annual conference the Board of Trustees authorized the immediate inauguration and vigorous prosecution of an emergency Capital Funds Campaign to raise at least $500,000 necessary to meet the requirements of the Annie Merner Pfeiffer bequest. Additional urgency was provided by the fact that building costs were rising and steadily pushing upward the amount necessary to erect the library and the two other buildings of equal cost required by the Pfeiffer gift. In the midst of this planning the trustees proceeded with the erection of the maintenance building.

The firm of A. Ivan Pelter and Associates of Ludington, Michigan, was engaged to conduct the Capital Funds Campaign. In the spring of 1949, Mr. Pelter reported that he had established headquarters on the second floor of the gymnasium, that he anticipated a prospect list of 25,000 to 30,000 persons, and that it would require six men working forty weeks to visit 24,000 prospects.

In view of the urging of Mr. Pelter that the beginning of construction would aid the campaign and of similar prodding by Garfield Merner, one of the executors of the Pfeiffer Estate, President Scarborough early in 1949 sought the advice of Dr. John O. Gross, executive secretary of the General Board of Education of The Methodist Church, trustee of the

Pfeiffer bequest. It was the opinion of Dr. Gross that if two dormitories were erected costing $150,000 each, they would meet the condition of Mrs. Pfeiffer's gift. However, the money for the library would not be available until the buildings were erected and funds raised to match the Pfeiffer money.

Within a year the Pelter organization reported that the Capital Funds Campaign was nearing completion. Their canvassers had made 30,000 calls and had secured 8,635 pledges. Results of the campaign were promising enough that Dr. Scarborough was able to report that the annual conference Board of Education had prepared a resolution to be presented to the annual conference authorizing the college to proceed with its building program, to borrow the money necessary to proceed and to pledge such part of the college property as would be required for security. Inasmuch as enough money had been raised for only one men's dormitory it was decided to erect one unit for men and the Loar Hall of Music and Fine Arts. In addition, the trustees authorized President Scarborough to negotiate with the officials in charge of the Federal Housing Act for funds to build a second unit of the men's dormitory. With the needed funds in sight, contracts were signed with the A. Farnell Blair Company, Inc., in the amount of $670,949.49 for the Annie Merner Pfeiffer Library, the L. L. Loar Hall of Music and Fine Arts, and the first unit of the men's dormitory which was subsequently named Fleming Hall. The Blair Company was unable to fulfill the terms of the contract and the construction was completed by the Byrum Construction Company of Wheeling, West Virginia. All three buildings were put into use between September 1952, and May 1953. Before these buildings were completed the Board of Trustees reaffirmed the original total Capital Funds goal of $2,000,000 and mapped out a future building goal including the second unit of the men's dormitory, the Calvin A. West Chapel, and a student center building.

Mr. James I. Ling was secured in 1950 as assistant to the president to complete the Capital Funds Campaign. Eventually the fund reached approximately $850,000 including the amount raised by "The Boys' Dormitory Building Fund" under the guidance of Dr. Fleming. Efforts to add to the fund or to collect on subscriptions ceased about June 1956.

In the planning stages of the library it was felt that some memorial should be placed there which would commemorate the material and spiritual union of the three branches of Methodism and which would be at the same time a testimony of love and appreciation for Bishop James Straughn of the Pittsburgh Area who had given strength, leadership and affection to the cause of West Virginia Wesleyan College. A bronze memorial plaque was struck from the picture of Bishops James H. Straughn, John M. Moore and Edwin Holt Hughes taken at the final session of the General Conference of the Methodist Episcopal Church South held at Birmingham, Alabama, at which the Plan of Union for the uniting of the three branches of the Methodist Church was ratified. Mr. Julian H. Harris of Atlanta, Georgia, executed the work at a cost of $8,000 and the Claude Worthington Benedum Foundation donated the funds for it. The plaque and the following inscription prepared by Bishop Straughn were placed in the first floor lobby of the library in 1953:

The Methodist Church

This plaque commemorates the formation of the Methodist Church. The three Chairmen, representing their churches, standing with interlocking hands are a symbol of the union which was consummated at the Uniting Conference, Kansas City, Missouri, 1939, with the plan of Union as the constitution of the new Church and with the adoption of a Book of Discipline.

This union of nearly 8,000,000 members healed the wounds of division of more than a hundred years within the Methodist family and affirmed that Methodists indeed are one people.

May God be praised.

In 1953 Mr. Clyde O. Law, chairman of the Board of Trustees, presented to the college the portraits of John Wesley and Francis Asbury which hang in the lobby of the library. In 1954 the board authorized Mr. Law to develop a project known as "Portraits of the Presidents." In the succeeding years the project, financed largely through contributions solicited by Mr. Law, resulted in the collection of portraits of all the presidents and deans of Wesleyan. To this collection have been added the portraits of a number of members of the faculty whose names have been synonymous with Wesleyan over the last quarter of a century—Dr. Ralph Brown, Dr. Lewis Chrisman, Dr. Nicholas Hyma, and Mr. "Cebe" Ross. The entire collection hangs in the library.

With the building program completed it was ascertained that seating, eating and sleeping facilities were adequate to entertain the West Virginia

Annual Conference of The Methodist Church. Supported by a resolution of the Chamber of Commerce of Buckhannon, an invitation was extended to the conference to meet at the college in 1953. Under the leadership of Mr. Ling the districts of the annual conference contributed $19,534.62 to a project known as "Chairs for Atkinson Chapel." This amount paid for new chairs and a new floor for the chapel. Since 1953 the conference has met annually at Wesleyan.

The mopping-up operations of the recent building program were scarcely completed when Dr. Scarborough presented to the Board of Trustees in March 1954, a recommendation for the creation of a "Special Sub-Committee on Policy and Planning" which would take into account the fact that Wesleyan would celebrate its 75th anniversary in 1965 and would be responsible for planning a long-range development program with this date in mind. The board adopted this resolution and another which authorized the purchase of the "Tannery Property." The property which lay east of the campus to the Buckhannon River was purchased for $14,000 with $5,000 provided by the Claude Worthington Benedum Foundation and other gifts. The property was designated "The Benedum Field" and was set aside for expanded outdoor athletic facilities.

The Policy and Planning Committee included J. Roy Price, Clyde O. Law, President Scarborough, A. G. Shannon, and G. J. Stallings. The committee produced a ten-year program to be achieved, so far as possible, by 1965. Under the heading of Student Body and Faculty, the program proposed that the student body be increased to 900, a number arrived at in the light of current long-range predictions of future college enrollment, and that the faculty be augmented as needed on the basis of an ultimate student-faculty ratio of twenty to one.

In the categorizing of immediate needs the program recommended that a new science building be erected as soon as it could be financed to provide for the Departments of Chemistry and Physics, and that housing for men be expanded to provide for an additional one hundred fifty students with lounge facilities and with dining facilities in the dormitory or elsewhere on campus.

Other needs suggested by the program included a new residence for women; the erection of the West Chapel; a new student center; a field house; equipment for the new buildings; the renovation of the Lynch-Raine Administration Building, the Haymond Science Hall and possibly the Old Music Hall; the landscaping of the campus; and an increase of the endowment to at least $2,500,000. The program also called for the inauguration of a "West Virginia Wesleyan Diamond Jubilee" campaign to raise the funds needed for the contemplated expansion.

The Board of Trustees adopted the program. At the same time it authorized application for a loan to the HHFA for the second men's residence. The loan was approved March 1, 1955. A year later the president was authorized to apply to HHFA for a loan of $600,000 for a residence hall for women. The men's dormitory was completed in 1958 at a cost of $593,000 and was named McCuskey Hall.

At the spring meeting of the Board of Trustees in 1956, Dr. Scarborough announced that Wesleyan would receive $97,900 from the Ford Foundation grant to hospitals, privately supported colleges and medical schools, the income from the grant to be used over a period of at least ten years to raise faculty salaries. Dr. Scarborough held that Wesleyan had a moral obligation to abide by the desire of the foundation that the gift would be used as a challenge to raise matching funds. Wesleyan ought to put a like amount in its endowment fund to underwrite faculty salaries. At the same time he noted that Wesleyan was one of fifty colleges selected by the Union Carbide Educational Foundation to participate in its scholarship program to the extent of four annual stipends of $500 to be awarded students planning careers in business, science or teaching. A like amount would be placed in the general budget of the college and the scholarship advisor would receive a stipend of $200.

Financial support of the college by the West Virginia Annual Conference increased pursuant to the action of the General Conference of 1952 which adopted a program of support for higher education based upon a program of 50 cents per member per year for schools and colleges and 15 cents per year for the Wesley Foundation. As of 1955 Dr. Scarborough reported that the annual conference was contributing 20 cents per member to the current budget and had been giving 37 cents per member over the past six years to the Capital Funds Program.

In terms of property expansion, the improvement of the school's financial posture, the advancement of its standing among the standard accrediting agencies, and the relationship of the school to the church, the years 1940-56 stand out as the most productive and creative era in the history of Wesleyan to that point. In the course of these developments other phases of the life and work at the school proceeded at a steady pace.

In 1942 the Nucleus Club, an honorary biology society, constructed a ten- by sixteen-foot greenhouse at the rear of the Science Hall. The money was raised by a student, Harold Almond, now a physician in Buckhannon, West Virginia, and the construction was supervised by Walter Kohlheim, now a surgeon in Parkersburg, West Virginia. Construction was done by students. The greenhouse was the first new structure erected on campus since the expansion of Agnes Howard Hall in 1928.

The Home Economics Cottage was dedicated November 19, 1942. This two-story brick cottage on Barbour Street was designed to afford opportunity for practice in home management. It was subsequently named for Miss Edna Jenkins, the donor.

In 1943 Mr. Harvey Harmer, a trustee of Wesleyan and president of the West Virginia Methodist Historical Society, announced that the annual conference had chosen Wesleyan as the repository for its official records. Upon completion of the Annie Merner Pfeiffer Library one room on the main floor was named the Methodist Room and a library of the records of the society was established therein. The District Superintendent's report to the annual conference in 1943 noted with approval that Wesleyan had just established a Department of Religious Education for the purpose of training capable church secretaries, directors of religious education and to broaden further the training of pre-ministerial students.

The impact of World War II was brought dramatically to the campus when early in March 1943, there arrived a contingent of officers and trainees subsequently organized as the 49th College Training Detachment (Aircrew). Students in Agnes Howard Hall were vacated and moved to living quarters in town in order to provide living space and staff offices for the detachment. Classrooms were provided using available space in the music hall, the gymnasium and by increased use of other facilities. The trainees were fed in a basement hall in the gymnasium. The college obtained sole use of the flying field on Brushy Fork for the training of the detachment. In addition to the men being trained for combat service, the college also maintained a program for training aides to draftsmen, engineers and chemists at Wright Field, Dayton, Ohio. A short, intensive course was provided for cadet nurses in training at St. Mary's Hospital in Clarksburg. The training of aircrew cadets ended June 1944, the program for Wright Field aides was closed at the end of the war, the courses for cadet nurses were given during the summer terms of 1944 and 1945. Seven hundred seventy-four aircrew cadets, four hundred eighty-seven aides, and seventy-eight cadet nurses were registered in these programs. The courses offered were regular college courses modified according to the suggestions of military educational directors in order to meet the needs of the program. On February 29, 1946, in cooperation with the Air Technical Command Service of the United States Air Force, Wesleyan inaugurated a twelve-month course of training on the college level for veterans interested in placement as engineering aides in the laboratories at Wright Field. The program was designed to train a minimum of one hundred fifty men.

In 1945 Dean Schoolcraft reported the expansion and diversification of offerings in the field of religious education, the strengthening of offerings in Home Economics to meet the standards of the American Dietetics Association, and in the Department of Music to conform to the standards of the National Association of Schools of Music. During the year the American Council on Education, Commission on Teacher Education, established at Wesleyan the first and only National Teacher's Examination Center in West Virginia.

The Dorothy Lee Scholarship Fund for overseas students was inaugurated during the school year 1945-46. The immediate need for the fund was the financing of the education of a Chinese girl at Wesleyan, Julia B. Cheng, a daughter of Dr. James Cheng of Shanghai and his wife Dorothy Lee who graduated from Wesleyan in the class of 1927. The ultimate objective of the fund was the creation of a permanent organization to render future assistance to other overseas students attending Wesleyan. While many persons have contributed to the fund the benefactions of Miss Edna Jenkins and the efforts of Dr. Roy McCuskey, prime mover in the establishment of the fund, have contributed materially to the continuing success of the venture. Dr. McCuskey has provided that any funds realized from the sale of his autobiography, *All Things Work Together for Good to Them that Love God,* beyond the cost of its publication, are to be placed in the Dorothy Lee Scholarship Fund.

In 1947 a one-story frame structure known as the Student Union was erected between the gymnasium and Loar Hall by the Federal Works Administration. The building, known as the Student Center of Wesleyan or SCOW, provided a lounge, fountain service, some offices, a health center, book store, recreation room and a study hall.

A gift in 1947 of $17,500 from the General Board of Education of the

Rockefeller Foundation provided partial salary for a sociologist for three years, funds for a library collection in the social sciences, a collection for the general library and equipment for the library. At the same time the Board of Missions and Church Extension of The Methodist Church announced annual support for the employment of a full-time person to work in the area of the rural church.

In 1948 a radio station for the broadcasting of student and faculty programs was put in operation on the fourth floor of Haymond Hall. The facility was operated in connection with a radio station at Weston owned and operated by an alumnus of the college.

Acting on a recommendation presented at the initiative of the Administration Committee the Board of Trustees voted March 3, 1949, to admit to West Virginia Wesleyan College qualified Negroes as regular students pursuing courses leading to degrees. A number of trustees objected to the action on the grounds that it was unnecessary inasmuch as nothing in the charter, by-laws or traditions of the school barred any member of any race from Wesleyan who met the moral and educational requirements for admission. In the light of this fact the action of the board might cause embarrassment to members of a group thus particularized. Further, it was objected that the action had been taken without any preliminary study or consideration, and, therefore, the timing of the action and its legality was questioned. It was suggested also that the raising of the issue might jeopardize the position of the school among constituents in and out of the church who still held to the traditional attitude on the Negro question. A motion to rescind the decision of the board and to advise the director of admissions that race was no barrier to admission or graduation from West Virginia Wesleyan College was defeated, and the original action stood.

During the years 1951-52, Wesleyan, along with many schools throughout the country, dropped football as an intercollegiate sport because of the lack of manpower arising out of the Korean conflict, the high cost of fielding a team, and a lack of scholarships for athletes. During this period coach Cebe Ross served as alumni secretary and director of admissions. Football was resumed in the fall of 1953.

An article in *Science,* May 11, 1951, entitled "The Origins of American Scientists" and a similar article in *Scientific American,* July 1951, entitled "The Origin of United States' Scientists" showed that Wesleyan stood in thirty-seventh place among the top fifty colleges in America in the production of scientists. Wesleyan was the only institution in West Virginia thus recognized and one of a few schools in the South. Credit for this achievement was given largely to Dr. Nicholas Hyma. The September-October 1951, issue of *Christian Education,* a journal published by The Methodist Church, listed Wesleyan as the number-one school in the nation in terms of Methodist pre-theological students.

At a cost of approximately $60,000 Agnes Howard Hall underwent extensive renovation in 1952. A new electrical system and fixtures were installed, walls were repainted, new plumbing was installed in the original wing, and all the old furniture and draperies were replaced.

In 1952 Wesleyan participated in the formation of the West Virginia Foundation of Independent Colleges. The foundation was incorporated in 1954. The objectives of the foundation were to interpret to the public the purposes, functions and needs of the member schools; to solicit support from business and industry operating in West Virginia and from interested individuals and organizations; to make a united approach to foundations or other groups interested in regional studies and area projects which seemed likely to make a contribution to the whole American scene; and to distribute funds received among the member institutions.

Mr. Ling was elected vice-president of Wesleyan in 1953, a position which he filled until his retirement in 1962.

In 1953 the name of the administration building was officially designated the Lynch-Raine Administration Building in honor of Judge Charles W. Lynch of Clarksburg, West Virginia, and the Honorable John Raine of Rainelle, West Virginia, both of whom had been chairmen of the Board of Trustees and benefactors of Wesleyan.

A Counselling Program long urged by the North Central Association was set up in 1954 with Dr. Florence Schaper as chairman, Mr. John D. Shaver as Dean of Men and Miss Nellie Wilson as Dean of Women. Mr. Sidney Davis was named College Chaplain. Dr. Scarborough reported the recent inauguration of programs in nursing, engineering and forestry as cooperative ventures with other colleges and universities.

Dean Schoolcraft announced in 1955 that for the first time since Wesleyan introduced its testing program Wesleyan freshmen had reached the national average on entrance examinations.

In 1956 Wesleyan was selected as the training center in the Northeast Jurisdiction for Methodist Youth Caravans; Mr. Clyde O. Law presided for the last time as chairman of the Board of Trustees after serving on the board for thirty-seven years and was succeeded as chairman by Mr. E. Ray Jones of Oakland, Maryland; Dr. Scarborough resigned as president on August 14, 1956, and Dean Schoolcraft was designated acting president. With characteristic humor Dr. Schoolcraft announced that his one ambition was to serve the shortest term of any acting president.

V

THE ERA OF EXPANSION

The years 1956 to the present can be characterized by the term expansion—expansion of student body and faculty, educational opportunities, physical plant, budget and long-range plans. Some facets of the expansion represent the meeting of needs long deferred. Other aspects of the expansion are part of the dream of a future Wesleyan equipped to meet the growing demand for education on the college level.

Dr. Stanley H. Martin came to the presidency of Wesleyan during the latter months of the 1956-57 academic year. Dr. Martin was born August 25, 1912, at Edina, Missouri. He attended high school in Quincy, Illinois, and in 1936 graduated from Quincy College with the degree of Bachelor of Arts. From Boston University he received the degrees of Bachelor of Sacred Theology and the Master of Arts in 1939, and the degree of Doctor of Philosophy in 1954. Adrian College conferred on Dr. Martin the honorary degree of Doctor of Divinity in 1954.

Dr. Martin was licensed to preach by the Methodist Episcopal Church in 1929, ordained Deacon in 1938 and Elder in 1941. He was a member in full connection with the New England Conference from 1950 to 1957. He has been a member of the West Virginia Conference since 1957.

From the beginning, Dr. Martin's career has been involved closely with the educational enterprise. He served as assistant pastor and minister to students at the University of Iowa, Iowa City, in 1941 and 1942; chaplain and professor of psychology at Simpson College, Indianola, Iowa, from 1942 to 1944; professor of religious education in the School of Theology and University Chaplain at Boston University, 1944-50. He served from 1950 to 1957 as Executive Secretary of the Departments of Student Loans, Scholarship and Personnel of the General Board of Education of The Methodist Church, Nashville, Tennessee.

In an early report to the Board of Trustees, Dr. Martin suggested three basic concerns which needed attention. These included the need to clarify the objectives of the college, the need for a comprehensive study and appraisal of the total curriculum of the college, and the need to develop a master plan for the campus.

The basic aim of Wesleyan to produce competent, cultured, Christian persons was clear. However, some dynamic, unifying force which would help implement this aim was badly needed. Such a force, he suggested, should involve an approach to life that is comprehensive yet devoid of dogmatism, contemporary yet historically sound. How to project such a philosophy of education should be a major concern of the college community.

With regard to the curriculum, special attention should be given to essential courses, improved methods of teaching, the enrichment of offerings, the utilization of national leadership in order to avoid narrowness and sectionalism, experimentation in new ways of communication, research, and experimentation in every phase of the academic program.

Finally, a program of building and finance to house and undergird the total effort of the college was imperative. The program should include a master plan for the campus and a development office to implement the plan. Among facilities urgently needed Dr. Martin listed a new science building, a student center, a chapel, and apartments for married students.

Steps were taken during 1957 and 1958 to further define and implement these needs. These included a survey of the total program of the college, and the development in detail by a Long Range Planning Committee of projects to be completed through 1965. The projects reflected in large part the suggestions advanced by the report of the Policy and Planning Committee of the previous administration.

The survey of the program of the college was authorized by the University Senate of The Methodist Church at the request of President Martin and the Board of Trustees. Dr. John O. Gross, General Secretary of the Division of Educational Institutions of the Board of Education of The Methodist Church, appointed the committee: Richard N. Bender, Secretary of the Division of Educational Institutions of the Board of Education of The Methodist Church; Everett L. Walker, Associate Director; Myron F. Wicke, Director of the Section of Secondary and Higher Education of the Board of Education of The Methodist Church; Emil Leffler, Dean of Albion College; and John Pepin, Treasurer of Drew University. The report of the committee was received by Wesleyan in May 1958.

With regard to the faculty, the survey noted a fine spirit of loyalty to the college. The number of earned doctorates and Master of Arts degrees held by the thirty-five members of the teaching staff compared

99

favorably with national averages and similar institutions. Faculty salaries constituted a major problem. While comparing favorably with other institutions in West Virginia, the Wesleyan median salary was still lower than most institutions outside the state. However, the retirement plan and other fringe benefits placed Wesleyan in the forefront of comparable schools.

Among the problems involving the program of instruction which required attention, the survey listed the need for eliminating one-man departments; reducing the number of courses offered; adjusting the size of classes, including those which were too large and those which were too small; reducing the instructional load and number of hours taught by the individual professor. The failure to include a foreign language within the range of possible use in the core curriculum was noted as a singular weakness. More needed to be done to encourage faculty research and writing. Faculty housing or assistance by the college to faculty in purchasing homes was noted as a foreseeable necessity.

The need for a study of the present use and future expansion of the library was suggested by the survey as an immediate concern. Though comparatively new, the library was already inadequate in terms of seating capacity, work space and other facilities. The circulation of books compared favorably with other institutions. Moderate increases in library expenditures were needed.

Wesleyan's role as a Christian liberal arts college was examined thoroughly by the Survey Committee, and a number of recommendations were made to strengthen the religious emphasis. Faculty should be encouraged to read materials in the field of religion in higher education, eminent scholars in the field should be brought to the campus, and faculty members should be encouraged and assisted to attend conferences centering on the Faculty Christian Movement. These strategies should aim at faculty involvement in informal and penetrating discussion of the Christian goals of the institution.

Wesleyan also needed a meaningful program for helping students to relate the insights of religion and philosophy to their total religious experience and to the practical problems of contemporary life.

The committee further recommended the formation of a religious life council representing the entire college community. The primary function of the committee would be to develop a basic philosophy for religious life activities at Wesleyan and to implement this philosophy by

100

long-range planning. The council would correlate all religious activities on campus.

While commenting favorably on the student personnel program, the survey recommended the consolidation and direction of the work in a centralized office with one administrator responsible for the total program. The report also advised the continuation of the current admissions policy, the establishment of a testing center with provisions for assisting faculty in making a maximum use of test scores, the improvement of the health center and the enlargement of infirmary space, and the development of the placement service in a central office with credentials for each student on file.

The long-range plans for the development of the campus were lauded by the survey report. It noted that a rule of thumb used by authorities on educational finances suggested that for every dollar invested in new plant facilities, the equivalent of the income from another dollar is needed to maintain the facility properly. However, it mentioned that Wesleyan's needs were so pressing that it would have to follow a less conservative policy with faith that the church and friends of the college would provide funds for maintenance.

With regard to plant expansion, the committee believed that top priority should be given to a new science building, a student union building, and a chapel. The percentage of students housed on campus should be raised, and this would necessitate new residence halls.

Additional endowment was listed as a must in order to offset the considerable reliance of the college on tuition and fees to meet its budgetary needs.

A major need, according to the survey, was for a development office under strong leadership to plan and carry out a systematic program of public relations and fund raising. The office should correlate all work in public relations, fund raising, publicity, alumni relations, and publications.

Surveys and committee reports generally are read and then filed away for future reference. But, in this instance, the report of the survey committee has been taken seriously, and in the intervening years a considered effort has been made to implement the recommendations.

Early in 1959 the college chaplain, Mr. Sidney Davis, took the first steps toward organizing the recommended Religious Life Council. With the assistance of faculty and students, these efforts were consummated the

101

following academic year with the organization of the Religious Life Council composed of representatives of the Methodist Student Movement, Kappa Phi, Sigma Theta Epsilon, the chaplains of all fraternities and sororities, and representatives of the faculty. Committees of the Council include the Special Religious Activities Committee, the Christian Emphasis Week Committee, the Chapel Committee and the Vespers Committee.

The Faculty Christian Fellowship was introduced to the campus in the fall of 1959. The fellowship, an informal and unstructured group of professors and administrative officers, meets on occasion for discussion of the ramifications of Christian higher education. This effort received its initial impetus at the opening faculty retreat in 1959 during which a day was spent discussing Dr. Elton Trueblood's book *The Idea of a College*. Since that time the fellowship has met and engaged in conversation with a number of distinguished Christian scholars including Dr. Elton Trueblood, Dr. J. B. Rhine, Dr. Laurence Lacour, Dr. Nels F. S. Ferre, Dr. Harold Schilling, Dr. Everett Tilson, Dr. Keith Irwin, and others.

During the summer of 1959 a Student Personnel Center was established in the area formerly occupied by the dining room of Agnes Howard Hall at a cost of $3,991.53. The center houses the offices of the dean of students, the dean of men, director of student aid and placement, the dean of women, the head counselor, and the secretarial office providing a secretarial pool and accumulative student records. In addition, the center provides a placement service and a vocations library. The dean of students was given responsibility for the direction of all student personnel activities, the health center, the counselling service, student housing, and all extra-curricular activities. The SCOW (Student Center of Wesleyan) which had been operated under the independent control of a student governing board was placed under this office also.

The health center in Agnes Howard Hall was also expanded and refurnished. In 1964 the former residence of the president at 68 College Avenue was converted to a health center and infirmary. Dr. Harold Almond was employed to work with Dr. Robert Chamberlain, the college physician. Both men practice in Buckhannon and are graduates of Wesleyan.

Under the leadership of President Martin the program outlined for long-range development became a continuing matter of study. The need for land for campus expansion led to the creation in 1957 of a committee of the Board of Trustees with authority to purchase property and land adjacent to the campus as it became available, provided funds were at hand for such purchase or the rental value of the property would amortize the purchase. The ultimate objective was the acquisition of all the land adjacent to the campus extending from Camden Avenue to the Buckhannon River. During the past several years the college has been engaged in serious negotiation with the Cumberland and Allegheny Gas Company for the purchase of its shops on Camden Avenue for use as a maintenance center.

In 1958 a plan for long-range development totaling $10,092,000 to be achieved by 1965 was presented to the Board of Trustees. Eventually, a plan in depth was adopted which included needed campus expansion, new buildings, the renovation and remodelling of existing facilities, additional endowment for the enlarged plant, endowment for ten faculty chairs, endowment for scholarships, a central heating plant, parking facilities, athletic facilities, and landscaping of the campus. These projects, plus furnishings, added up to a long-range plan of development totaling $22,283,000.

At the same time, the architectural firm of Larson and Larson of Winston-Salem, North Carolina, was employed by the college. The following spring, the firm exhibited a general plan of campus expansion and development based on the work of the Long Range Planning Committee. The Board of Trustees approved the plan with the provision that each project would be subject to specific approval when proposed and as funds became available. In 1962 a moveable scale model of the projected campus, housed in a plastic bubble, was constructed by Larson and Larson who also donated a large portion of the cost of $8,000.

In view of the long-felt need for a new chapel, upon recommendation of President Martin, an appeal was made to the West Virginia Annual Conference to include the raising of funds for a chapel and religion center in its quadrennial program for 1960-64. The annual conference included the sum of $1,000,000 for this purpose in the Faith in Action program for the quadrennium. Also in 1960 the West Virginia Annual Conference approved a Capital Funds Campaign of $2,500,000 for the student center, the science building and other needed facilities. The president was given authority by the Board of Trustees to appoint a special committee to help raise money for the gymnasium.

Early in 1959 initial steps were taken toward establishing a develop-

103

ment office. In view of the fact that the survey report had urged the college to seek professional help in this enterprise, the American City Bureau was employed for one year to assist in establishing the fund raising activities of the school on a professional basis.

In the fall of 1960 President Martin announced that Mr. Leonard Bucklin had been employed as vice-president of the college to succeed Mr. James Ling who retired in July. Mr. Bucklin, with the help of Mr. Ling who continued to work on a part-time basis in the area of wills and estates, assumed responsibility for the establishment and direction of the development office. In addition, Mr. Bucklin was given administrative responsibility for the Audio-Visual Department and the weekly radio program; the Public Information Office which handled newspaper, radio and television releases; the Alumni Office and the Publications Office. Much of Mr. Bucklin's effort was channeled into preparation for the direction of the Diamond Jubilee Campaign, the initial capital funds phase of the Long Range Development Plan. In 1964 Dr. Robert B. Nemeschy succeeded Mr. Bucklin as vice-president.

Dr. J. Roy Price, a trustee recently retired from the Union Carbide Company, was employed in 1962 as a part-time representative of the college to contact foundations, corporations, friends and alumni of Wesleyan on the East Coast. In 1964 Mr. A. T. Artzberger was employed also on a part-time basis to cultivate the field in West Virginia and Western Pennsylvania.

The plans and timetable for the campaign for capital funds, to be known as the Diamond Jubilee Campaign, called for the effort to begin January 1, 1962. By October of that year solicitations had been conducted among the college personnel and in the cities of Buckhannon, Clarksburg, Weston, Charleston, Parkersburg, Morgantown, and Wheeling in the state of West Virginia. By May 1963, the state of West Virginia, which had been divided into thirteen areas, had been solicited. Outside the state solicitations were conducted in the following areas: Baltimore-Washington, Connecticut, Florida, Iowa, Massachusetts, New York-New Jersey, Ohio, Pennsylvania-Philadelphia, Pennsylvania-Pittsburgh, and Cumberland, Maryland.

Mr. Bucklin reported limited success in the campaign and noted the need for a substantial challenge gift. A committee of the Board of Trustees in reviewing the progress of the campaign identified a number of factors militating against the project including difficulty encountered in securing solicitors, and a disappointing response among alumni and many constituents. However, the committee noted, the campaign had produced some good results. The literature printed for the effort had been outstanding and had done much to create a new and finer image of Wesleyan. The organizational structure of the campaign had been of high caliber. The work of Dr. Roy Price in contacting foundations and corporations was judged to hold productive promise for the future. Results of the campaign to date were found to be encouraging; $425,000 had been pledged. Contacts had been made which would produce results in the future.

In retrospect, this initial phase of the Diamond Jubilee Campaign has been adjudged as having provided a valuable and needed interpretation of what Wesleyan has been as well as a projection of what Wesleyan hopes to be.

In the midst of these developments the expansion of the physical plant proceeded with the erection of three dormitories and a student center. The first dormitory for women to be erected since the building of Agnes Howard Hall was completed and occupied in the fall of 1959. The hall was erected by the John I. Vandergrift Company at a cost of $712,000, and $35,000 for the furnishings. The dormitory was originally named the Edna Jenkins Hall, but this was subsequently changed to Jenkins Hall at the request of Miss Jenkins. The dining hall was named the Benedum Dining Hall in honor of Michael L. Benedum and Dr. Paul B. Benedum. The lounge was named for Miss Jessie B. Trotter in honor of Miss Trotter who taught Latin and mathematics in the seminary and college from 1896 to 1912.

The third residence hall for men was completed in 1962 by C. H. Jimison and Sons of Huntington, West Virginia at a cost of $839,373 for the building and $38,000 for the furnishings. The hall was named for Dr. Carl G. Doney, president of Wesleyan from 1907 to 1915.

A third residence hall for women was completed during the summer of 1963 on the corner of Meade and Camden Avenue. The hall, which has not been named, houses two hundred women and contains four chapter rooms provided for sororities on a rental basis. The residence was erected by the Fogleman Construction Company at a cost of $1,032,703. The furnishings cost $39,753. Additions to the dining rooms of Jenkins Hall and McCuskey Hall were completed in 1964 at a cost of $108,785,

105

and the corridor walls and ceilings of McCuskey Hall were renovated at a cost of $95,920.

The long-standing need for a student center was brought into the realm of reality with a gift of $300,000 in 1960 by the Claude Worthington Benedum Foundation. The balance of the $1,150,000 for financing the building came from a self-liquidating HHFA loan which is being repaid with a student center fee. An additional gift from the Benedum Foundation of $100,000 in 1962 made possible the furnishing of the center. In 1964 the Foundation provided another $45,000 for air-conditioning and landscaping. The center was named the Benedum Campus Community Center. Facilities in the center include a swimming pool, post office, coffee shop, book store, radio studios, student organization offices, music listening rooms, six bowling lanes, game room, social hall, faculty lounge, parlor, a roof deck area for dining and dancing, and locker facilities for commuting students.

The center opened February 2, 1963, with the Reverend Mr. James Stansbury as director and Mrs. Martin Talbott as temporary program director. Mrs. Clifford L. Summers of Buckhannon became permanent program director in April 1963. The responsibility for planning a varied program of social, cultural and recreational activities was vested in a Campus Center Program Board working in cooperation with the center director and the program director. The initial board included students John Young, chairman; James Marsh, vice-chairman; Rebecca Emch, secretary; Scott Wright, treasurer; Richard McCullough and Linda Burley, chairmen of recreation; William Smith and Martha Alderson, chairmen of cultural activities; Larry Dillon and Brenda Blake, chairmen of social activities. Miss Jane Schnabel and Dr. Kenneth M. Plummer were faculty members of the board.

With the opening of the center, the old SCOW was remodelled for use as classrooms and laboratories by the Departments of Psychology and Education and the Testing and Evaluation Service.

In 1964 initial steps were taken to establish a 3000-watt FM radio station in the center. A transmitter and antenna were obtained, and funds are being solicited for the remainder of the equipment. Hopefully, the station will begin broadcasting the first semester of the academic year 1965-66.

The plan to build a central heating plant to replace "Old Smokey" which had done yeoman's service for nearly fifty years was consummated during the summer of 1964 with the construction of a plant below ground at the rear of Atkinson Chapel. The plant, using natural gas instead of coal, will provide heat for the buildings at the heart of the campus. Eventually it will be part of the connecting link between the new chapel and religion center and the Lynch-Raine Administration Building.

The Board of Trustees meeting October 1964, authorized President Martin to advertise for bids on the new chapel and religion center on or before March 15, 1965. The plans for this facility provide for a sanctuary which will seat eighteen hundred persons; classrooms; offices for the Division of Bible, Philosophy and Religion; and space for religious activities. The plans also include a meditation chapel which will be known as the West Chapel. The chapel, underwritten by a bequest made by Mary Lowe West in memory of her husband Calvin A. West, will be constructed consistent with the terms of the bequest. It is anticipated that the structure will be completed in time for the official celebration of the Diamond Jubilee in June 1966.

During the fall of 1961 the family of the late Arthur G. Shannon, Buckhannon merchant and trustee of the college from 1934-53, presented Wesleyan with the gift of a Schulmerich Carillon costing $24,825. The carillon, known as the "Shannon Bells," was installed in the tower of the Lynch-Raine Administration Building. It will be transferred to the new chapel and tied in with the organ console. The bell from the tower of the original seminary building will be placed in the steeple of the new chapel and tied in with the Shannon Bells.

The present status of the campaign for funds for further expansion of the physical plant provides hopeful signs that by the date of the official celebration the new science building either will be underwritten or under construction, and that funds for a new gymnasium will be in sight. It is estimated that the science building, including equipment, will cost approximately $1,879,000. Of this amount $947,830 has been pledged including gifts of $50,000 from the Richard King Mellon Foundation, $25,000 from the Mary Reynolds Babcock Foundation, Inc., $250,000 from Mr. and Mrs. Frank Christopher of Millwood, Virginia, and a $600,000 matching grant from the Claude Worthington Benedum Foundation, the largest single grant Wesleyan has received in its history. Authority has been given the president of the college to file an application with the State Commission on Higher Education for a Federal grant under the Educational Facilities Act of 1963 to be applied toward the construction of the new science building, the extension of the library, and the remodeling and improving of present classroom facilities.

The steady yearly growth of the student body and the faculty has created housing problems for both of these segments of the college community. The need for faculty housing on a short-term basis has been critical for a number of years. Pursuant to recommendation by President Martin, the Board of Trustees has approved also the construction of a fourth residence hall for women to house two hundred students, two residence halls for men to house fifty each, two married student apartments of twenty apartments each, and two faculty apartment buildings of eight apartments each. The hall for women will be located between the L. L. Loar and Family Building and the newest women's dormitory. It is hoped that the other buildings will be located, in keeping with the master plan for campus expansion, below Camden Avenue.

The expansion of the physical plant has been accompanied by advances in the educational program at Wesleyan. The more important changes have occurred in the areas of instructional facilities, academic standards, curricular innovations, and the growth of the faculty.

For many years the faculty at Wesleyan has been hampered by lack of instructional facilities. The limitations of the assumption, valid in itself, that good instruction is strictly a matter of relationship between student and teacher has been recognized, and Wesleyan is making a concerted effort to furnish instructors with the best in the way of a physical plant and teaching aids.

The intention to achieve high academic standards at Wesleyan has been hampered for many years for a number of reasons. Within the past half decade some gains have been made. In recent years there have been few waivers in regard to important graduation requirements. In the cases of the graduating classes of 1962-63 and 1963-64, not a single waiver was issued on the requirement of a 2.00 overall average at Wesleyan, as well as in the major and minor fields of study. In the past, through administrative action, Wesleyan has waived certain academic requirements so that athletes could participate in intercollegiate sports. There have been practically no exceptions made during the past several years, even though Wesleyan's requirements for participation in athletics are considerably higher than those of most other colleges in the state.

Wesleyan has had a rather traditional curriculum. Perhaps one reason for this curricular orthodoxy has been the extensive teacher training program and the close tie with the State Department of Education. This and other factors including limited facilities, finances and faculty have made experimentation in curriculum difficult. The area of language study is a case in point. After having dropped a traditional emphasis on classical and foreign languages, in part to attract students, Wesleyan is attempting now to expand the offerings in the hope that at some time during the next decade a modern foreign language may be required for the A.B. degree.

Another important dimension in Wesleyan's present development is in the area of international education. The growth of opportunities in this field has been accomplished in the area of curricular offerings, the acquisition of faculty members with foreign backgrounds, and the foreign student program. Wesleyan's participation in the Regional Council for International Education will strengthen this development. Wesleyan was the first college in West Virginia to join the council. A center for Latin American Studies has been established at Wesleyan under the direction of Mr. Frederick A. Peterson.

In the area of the natural sciences a number of developments have occurred during the last decade which carry on the tradition of excellence in this area of study which has been associated with the work of the late Dr. Nicholas Hyma. Dr. Hyma died at the beginning of the present administration, but he left a permanent mark on Wesleyan. He gained an enviable reputation for the number of students he persuaded to do graduate work in chemistry. He was the motivating spirit in the organization of the Benzene Ring and the crowning of the "Camphor King" at the annual breakfast of the organization during commencement. Dr. Hyma organized the Hyma Chemical Laboratory and was a leading coal analyst and authority on coal analysis in West Virginia. He lent encouragement and aid in the founding of the first student union in the basement of the Science Hall.

The new dimension in the program of the natural sciences which has developed during the last five years has come about with the material assistance of various national foundations.

In 1959 Wesleyan received for the first time a grant from the National Science Foundation. The grant of $50,000 was used to support a six-week summer institute for fifty junior high school teachers of science. A grant of $60,000 the following year enabled sixty teachers to attend the 1960 summer institute. During the same summer fifty exceptional high school students spent three weeks at Wesleyan learning about the scientific observations made during the International Geophysical Year. This program which was supported by a grant of $10,000 from the National Science Foundation was extended to four weeks in 1961 through a grant of $13,000.

A new type of summer program was initiated in 1961 with a grant of $20,000 from the National Science Foundation. For six weeks forty exceptional high school students were in residence at Wesleyan studying a new chemistry curriculum. Simultaneously, ten teachers were being trained to return to their high schools and teach the new curriculum in the fall. This program was repeated in 1962. During the 1963-64 academic year a similar program was carried out on Saturdays on an extension basis with forty students and twenty chemistry teachers from Kanawha County, West Virginia, participating. The National Science Foundation awarded Wesleyan $30,000 for a similar program during the summer of 1964 and for a follow-up program during the academic year 1964-65 in Huntington, Beckley and Clarksburg, West Virginia.

Also during the summer of 1964 twenty-seven high school students of high ability were brought to campus for a six-weeks institute designed for students with limited educational opportunities in physics. The program, again, was financed with a grant of $9,287 from the National Science Foundation. In this venture the new Physical Science Study Committee Curriculum for Physics was used. The Department of Physics has made application for a grant to underwrite a similar program for the summer of 1965.

Since 1958 Wesleyan has conducted each summer an Institute of American Studies. For five years the institute was supported financially by the Coe Foundation, and since 1963 the Claude Worthington Benedum Foundation has assumed one-half of the support. The institute, designed to provide public school teachers with a greater understanding of the American heritage, has brought to campus elementary and secondary teachers from West Virginia and surrounding states. Noted scholars from many universities have provided the instruction, each presenting one week of lectures in his field of specialization. The greatest emphasis has been placed on American history, but such fields as diplomacy, constitutional law, music, economics, and archeology have been included. Each summer one lecturer in the field of religion has been part of the offerings of the institute. In 1964 Wesleyan initiated a Center for American Studies under the direction of Dr. Dwight Mikkelson of the Department of History to assist in coordinating and directing attention to the various courses and programs of the college which have an essentially American emphasis.

A Department of Nursing was organized in 1961 under the direction of Miss George Rast after consultation with the West Virginia State Board of Examiners for Registered Nurses and with the nursing representative of the Board of Hospitals and Homes of The Methodist Church. The nursing program is being developed to offer an eight-semester course of study combining work in liberal arts with training in nursing. Graduates will receive a Bachelor of Science degree in Nursing. A coordinated program is offered by the department which includes academic work and classes in nursing; clinical experience in general nursing and in maternal and child nursing at the Union Protestant Hospital in Clarksburg, West Virginia; psychiatric nursing experience at the Weston State Hospital, Weston, West Virginia; public health nursing clinical experience through work with the Harrison County-Clarksburg Department of Public Assistance.

The Department of Nursing was approved on a year-to-year basis by the West Virginia State Board of Examiners for Registered Nurses until the first class graduated in 1965. At this time, the Department of Nursing becomes eligible to seek accreditation by the National League for Nursing.

A new departure in the program of religious education and teacher training was inaugurated with the establishment of a Kindergarten Laboratory in 1960 under the direction of Miss Helen Stealey. The school was planned to serve a dual purpose. It aimed at providing training for kindergarten teachers for both the public schools, where there has been a dearth of kindergartens and qualified teachers, and for the church, which has manifested a growing interest in providing opportunities for children on this level. The school also aimed to serve the community by providing a church-oriented kindergarten for children in the area surrounding Wesleyan. Each year the kindergarten has enrolled approximately twenty-five pupils and fifteen teacher trainees. Interest in the school already has outgrown the staff and facilities, so that expansion of the program is anticipated.

In connection with the school, a workshop or short-term laboratory school for in-service training of kindergarten teachers has been offered each summer. The summer program has drawn teachers from the Northeast Jurisdiction of The Methodist Church and has had an interdenominational clientele.

Further service to the church at large and to the community surrounding Wesleyan developed in 1961 when the Reverend Mr. Ralph Grieser was employed to direct a Town and Country Program jointly sponsored and supported by the college and the Methodist Board of National Missions, Town and Country Department. Mr. Grieser was given responsibility for supervising and improving the work of preministerial students, and for serving as a liaison person between the college and the church in West Virginia.

Much attention has been given to the program of teacher education. The Normal School, which served a useful purpose during the first four decades of the life of the school, was no longer listed after 1927-28. Students preparing to teach junior high and high school in the Department of Education were warned that they could expect to attend school for four and a half or five years in order to meet the requirements for certification and graduation. By 1935, however, a program had been worked out by which the prospective teacher could qualify for a teaching certificate and a B.A. degree with a major in education within four years and the required one hundred twenty-eight hours for graduation. This remained the pattern for almost thirty years.

In 1963 the faculty approved a teacher education program of a different nature. The emphasis was changed from one of an accumulation of credits to one of completion of a sequential program. A comprehensive self-study was initiated also in 1963 in preparation for membership in the National Council for Accreditation of Teacher Education. Presently a teacher education program embodying the latest requirements of the West Virginia State Board of Education is being prepared by a Committee on Teacher Education. The program, if approved by the faculty and the state board, will provide a five-year course of study culminating in a bachelor's and the M.A.T. (Master of Arts in Teaching) degrees. Only those students who complete the M.A.T. program will receive Wesleyan's endorsement as graduates of the teacher education program.

For the past five years special encouragement has been given to the faculty to engage in research and to promote research projects which would involve advanced undergraduate students. An annual budget of $1,000 has been established since 1960 to help support faculty research projects. Awards have been made by a Faculty Committee on Research.

Assistance has been given for such diverse enterprises as Dr. Howard Teeple's preparation of slide lectures on New Testament manuscripts; Dr. George Rossbach's study of the taxonomic botany and geographical distribution of plant species in West Virginia and Maine; Dr. Leonard Roberts' transcription and preparation for publication of his taped collection of folklore; Dr. Buell Agey's transcription and editing with analytical notes of folk music taped by Dr. Roberts; and Mr. Herbert Buhler's research on the Gestalt Visual Stimuli Project of the Department of Psychology, Sociology and Anthropology.

Grants from the Research Corporation and from the National Institute of Health in the aggregate of $3,000 enabled Mr. Stephen Tobey to conduct research in the properties of various chemical compounds. Dr. John Wright also received two grants of $1,000 each from the Research Corporation. In addition, Dr. Wright was awarded a grant of $15,000 from the National Science Foundation for research involving undergraduate students in the Chemistry Department plus a grant of $10,000 for equipment. Dr. Wright was also instrumental in procuring approximately $7,000 worth of equipment from the Atomic Energy Commission.

Dr. Albin Gilbert, Professor of Psychology, has completed a research project based on a technique of timed cross-examination. This project supported by a grant from the National Institute of Health is aimed at developing a method of personality analysis which will reveal specific areas of wholesomeness or of anxiety in personality.

The possibility of new dimensions in education and research opened up in 1964 when Wesleyan obtained a Burroughs 205 Electronic Digital Computer. The computer has a book value in the neighborhood of one quarter million dollars. The main computer, power supply, power control, control console, high speed paper punch and a Flexowriter were gifts of the Burroughs Corporation. The balance of the equipment was purchased by the college at salvage prices. The computer is housed in a building renovated for this purpose on the former Brake property at the corner of Meade Street and Camden Avenue. The Computer Center is under the direction of Dr. William Willis.

The computer will be used primarily as an educational tool to stimulate interest among students in programming and the possible uses of the machine by the departments of physics, chemistry, mathematics and business administration. However, it is expected that the use of the computer will spread to other departments. Already the Social Science Division has used the computer in connection with Dr. Albin Gilbert's research. The Testing and Evaluation Service will use it in analyzing the results of the college testing program. The registrar's office is developing a program which will use the computer to automate registration procedures. It is hoped that eventually the computer will provide a campus-wide data processing center, and a tool for research.

In its continuing effort to improve instruction and strengthen its curriculum, Wesleyan, during 1964-65, moved into the arena of new approaches of learning provided by the communication media. The faculty and administration under the leadership of Dr. Walter Brown made a beginning in the use of radio, tele-lecture, closed circuit TV, overhead projection, tape libraries and other modern learning devices. Through these media it is now possible to bring to campus outstanding professors, government leaders, scientists, and religious leaders from all parts of the globe. Wesleyan now envisions an educational media and learning center which will contain all segments of the modern communications process, so that all students might avail themselves of the materials and techniques for effective learning.

Ventures into new areas of study, experimentation and research, utilization of new media of instruction enrich and give depth to the educational program at Wesleyan, but they have not changed the basic pattern. Recognizing the need for such a change, Dr. Stanley Martin presented to the Board of Trustees and the college community on March 18, 1964, his proposal for a new approach to Wesleyan's total educational program. This program will be discussed in detail in another context.

Great teaching has been traditionally one of Wesleyan's virtues. For a number of years this teaching centered in a small core of dedicated teachers. Because of the great growth of the school over the past decade, and because of the nature of some of the larger departments, it has been difficult to acquire faculty persons within the limits of the salary scale. Nevertheless, the faculty has been expanded and strengthened both in terms of levels of accomplishment and in terms of skills and classroom functioning. The number of full-time faculty has increased from 31.5 in 1956 to 90 for 1964-65. Dean Strunk has suggested that the present faculty at Wesleyan ranks high in instructional sophistication, though it perhaps does not, at this point, contain the small dramatic core of teachers referred to traditionally in the college literature.

An integral element in any educational program is, of course, the

114

student. During the past twenty years the problem of recruitment has received special attention at Wesleyan. In 1944 before the influx of World War II veterans, the enrollment was 159 full-time students. Beginning in September 1945, veterans began arriving on campus, and the number of full-time students rose to 227. The peak of veteran enrollment came in 1948 when the student body numbered 790. From that point on as the number of veterans declined, the number of students also decreased until a low enrollment of 397 was registered in 1952.

In an effort to increase the size of the student body, Wesleyan turned to student referral agencies in New York and other large eastern and midwestern cities. Three agencies were in the service of the college: the Advisory Service in Private Schools and Colleges, the American Schools and Colleges Association, and the School and Advisory Center. During a period covering three years the agencies sent Wesleyan a total of 209 students.

The personnel in the admissions office was changed on November 1, 1956, and a totally new admissions program was inaugurated with Mr. Raymond Kiser in charge. At the end of the school year the contracts with all agencies were terminated. A concerted effort was launched among the alumni, ministers and other friends of the college for new students. Emphasis was placed upon the recruitment of more students from West Virginia. In addition, Wesleyan made a strong appeal to all Methodist churches in the Northeastern Jurisdiction. The response was such that enrollment began moving upward again. From 1957, when the full-time enrollment was 789, the number of full-time students has increased yearly to a high of 1439 for the opening of the 1964-65 school year. Planning for the school year 1965-66 is based on a projected student body of 1500. The recent burgeoning college enrollment has enabled Wesleyan to shift the emphasis from the drive to obtain numbers of students to more emphasis on the type of student it seeks.

A major problem for Wesleyan in recent years has been the consistent decline in the percentage of its total enrollment of students from West Virginia. Prior to World War II the percentage of students from West Virginia at Wesleyan ran as high as 70 per cent. Despite the fact that the number of students from West Virginia has increased, the percentage of the total student body has decreased from a high of 81 per cent in 1946-47 to a low of 32.1 per cent in 1962. This decline has been attributed to a number of factors, two of which have a special bearing on the problem. First, as the cost of attending Wesleyan has increased gradually to a present total of about $1800 per year, many potential students from West Virginia have found that they cannot attend Wesleyan for financial reasons. The per capita income of West Virginia has not kept pace with that of the nation as a whole, and students are turning to state-supported schools where costs are lower. Second, the population of West Virginia has shown a marked decline over the period from 1950 to 1960. The projected population trends predict that the state will continue to lose population until 1970 to the extent of at least another 17 per cent.

The implications of the population decrease for college enrollments have been felt by all institutions of higher learning in West Virginia. The number of college age young people in the state is not increasing at the same rate as the national average, and the number of West Virginia students entering West Virginia colleges has increased very little. Two colleges have been added to the total in the state in recent years. As a result of these factors, all colleges within the state, private or state supported, have been looking to other states for more students. The problem is further complicated by the fact that only 26 per cent of West Virginia high school graduates go on to any form of higher education, a figure well below the national average of 40 per cent. Of those who do pursue their education beyond high school, 15 per cent go out of the state. From 1958 to 1962 the number of West Virginia students going to West Virginia institutions of higher learning showed an increase of only 2,299. Divided equally among the 20 schools in the state, this would average an increase of slightly over two hundred for each over the five-year period. During the same years the number of out-of-state students enrolled in West Virginia colleges has more than doubled.

The admissions office at Wesleyan has made special efforts to recruit more students from West Virginia. The school year 1963-64 showed a .02 per cent increase over the previous year. However, the basic problem appears to be an economic one, and the solution awaits the development of new and increased sources of aid for this segment of the student body.

With the growth of the faculty and student body at Wesleyan attention has been focused on the library as central to the whole enterprise of education. Each year since the turn of the century the book collection has grown. The growth has conformed closely to the pattern of most college and university libraries which tend to double in size every 16 years. In 1937 there were 18,000 books in the library; now there are more than 60,000. It is anticipated that by the year 1975 there will be at least 100,000 volumes available for the Wesleyan student of that year. Although still small when compared with some institutional libraries, the Wesleyan library possesses a well-rounded book collection and an exceptional reference collection. For the last several years Wesleyan has been consistently in the forefront of West Virginia colleges in the circulation of books.

During the past decade a number of collections and grants have added materially to the resources of the library.

In 1957 a graduate of Wesleyan, Mr. Harry Byrer of Martinsburg, West Virginia, gave the initial contribution for the establishment of the Judge Samuel Woods Memorial Collection in memory of his grandfather, a founder and first president of the Board of Trustees of the seminary. Mr. Byrer has provided additional funds each year for the purchase of books in the field of Biblical studies and related areas.

Mr. C. A. Jones of Columbus, Ohio, a graduate of the seminary in 1904, has presented the library with a considerable segment of his Lincoln Collection. Mr. Jones occasionally augments the collection, and eventually his entire holdings will come to Wesleyan.

A grant of $10,000 from the Kellogg Foundation, with a matching gift from the General Board of Education of The Methodist Church, was received in 1961 for the purchase of books in the field of teacher education.

The Japanese Society contributed $250 in 1964 for the acquisition of books in Japanese history and culture.

The growth of the college during the last ten years has been accompanied by an expansion of the library facilities and staff. In 1953 the library was staffed by three full-time librarians; today there are nine. However, the college has already outgrown the present facilities, and the plans for long-range development provide for an enlarged building with space for 100,000 volumes, large work areas, and a seating capacity of at least 450 students.

It is not possible to measure the growth of an institution by its financial posture alone, but finances certainly provide one indication as to whether it is a dynamic or a static institution. The past decade shows expansion in all phases of the financial life of Wesleyan. Actual total expenses for the operation of the college have risen from $445,726 in 1954 to $2,113,457 in 1964. The budget for instructional salaries rose from $111,807 to $435,092. The library budget increased steadily from

$14,599 to $55,600 with a goal for this expenditure set at 5 per cent of the total budget exclusive of auxiliary enterprises. Student aid has jumped from $12,610 to $114,595 with 28 per cent of the student body receiving such aid.

Income from various sources has expanded also. The endowment has grown from $304,440 in 1954 to $1,460,155 in 1964. Income from endowment is currently $51,278 per year as compared with $23,042 in 1954. Over the decade scholarship endowment funds have increased from $84,509 to $277,247. Gifts and grants from industry, foundations and friends in the amount of $53,509 in 1954 amounted to $187,953 in 1964. The value of the plant and facilities stood at $1,403,813 in 1954, having doubled the figure of the previous year with the completion of the building program. The value of plant and facilities now stands at $6,373,298.

A significant development has been the steady growth of the support of Wesleyan by the West Virginia Annual Conference of The Methodist Church. Over a five-year period beginning in 1954, support by the conference averaged approximately $43,000 per year. In 1959 this amount more than doubled and has increased yearly to a present figure of $144,746 for 1963-64. Growing support by the Western Pennsylvania Conference between 1950 and 1964 has totaled $180,506.03. The same conference has pledge $250,000 for the years 1965 through 1968 for the Department of Nursing at Wesleyan. The Erie Conference contributed a total of $2,569 to Wesleyan in 1953 and again in 1960-62.

A further important development during the past decade has been in the area of alumni relations. Records concerning the founding of the alumni association are non-existent. Information gleaned from various college publications indicates that since the founding of the school there has been a continuous effort to relate the alumni to the institution. The June 1898, issue of the *Seminary Collegiate* refers to a meeting of the Alumni Association. The June 1901, issue mentions the annual alumni banquet to be held at commencement time. These banquets apparently have been an annual occasion down to the present.

Cultivation of the alumni during the early years was evidently done on an occasional and voluntary basis. An alumni office of sorts has been in existence at least since 1917, the year the first alumni directory was issued. However, the direction of the office was a part-time operation, since alumni affairs were the responsibility of a member of the staff who worked full time at another job. It was not until 1936-37 that an alumni secretary was listed as part of the college administration, though alumni secretaries were listed prior to this date including Carl V. Miller, 1922-26, who was also director of athletics, and Arthur E. Beckett, 1935-37. The list of alumni secretaries include Floyd N. Shaver, 1939-43; Hobart Beeghley, 1944-45; William D. Foster, 1946-50, also director of public relations; Cecil B. Ross, 1950-53, also director of athletics; Robert James Stansbury, 1954-59, also director of public relations and director of publications; Walter L. Collins, 1960-1965, also director of publications.

In 1946 President Scarborough strived for the establishment of an effective and separate alumni office with modern equipment for addressing and mailing. Dr. Scarborough felt that the college should take the initiative in organizing, supporting and maintaining the office. This suggestion was consummated in 1954 with the establishment of an alumni office in the Lynch-Raine Administration Building. In 1962 the office was moved to the Alumni House on the corner of Meade Street and College Avenue.

There were less than six active alumni chapters in 1954. Prior to this date alumni chapters were organized evidently only in those towns where Wesleyan teams participated in athletic competition, and the meetings of the chapters probably were held at the time of athletic contests. By 1960 there were thirty alumni chapters throughout the country, most of them meeting annually. In 1964 there were thirty-six chapters, seventeen located in West Virginia and nineteen out of state. Most chapters meet once each year, though a few meet only once every two or three years. Class meetings are held at commencement and homecoming, and each class has a reunion every five years.

The *College Bulletin* series which was first issued as a magazine in the late thirties was succeeded by the *Sundial,* the official alumni magazine first published in September 1955. These journals have been the official channel for alumni news and for getting information concerning the college to alumni. Frequent bulletins are issued also. Alumni directories have been published in 1917, but there is no available copy; in 1926, showing 1331 graduates of the seminary, academy, normal school and college; in 1947; in 1958, showing 5,628 alumni; and 1964, showing 6,232 alumni.

From the beginning the Alumni Association has worked through the college. Records of alumni giving are sparse and inadequate. For many years the treasurer's office and the office of the vice-president handled alumni giving. Today, through the cooperation of these offices and the alumni office, complete records are kept of annual alumni giving. This has increased considerably in recent years. In 1951-52 alumni gifts totaled $20,000. Alumni gave $64,000 in 1963-64.

The alumni are organized in the West Virginia Wesleyan College Alumni Association. The governing body of the Association is an Alumni Council consisting of twenty-four members elected by the council with the president of the college, the president of the Board of Trustees, and the alumni secretary as ex-officio members. The council has the responsibility of implementing any policies or programs suggested by the association which promote the object and purpose of the organization, that is, the interests and welfare of the association and the college. The council works to achieve close cooperation between the college and the association. Each year the council chooses not more than three graduates and non-graduates to receive Alumni Awards for outstanding service to the college. The Association also conducts an annual solicitation among alumni for funds which are channeled to the college.

In view of the interest of many alumni in a program of scholarship and student aid, the Alumni Council on May 10, 1962, established the West Virginia Wesleyan College Alumni Permanent Endowment Fund. Mr. Leslie D. Price, attorney, and Mr. Houston G. Young, broker, gave impetus to this development. Contributions to the fund are invested, and income from the investment is earmarked for scholarship and student aid, and for aid for college administrative purposes during periods of critical need. The fund is administered by a trust committee elected by the Alumni Council.

Many aspects of the life of an educational institution, such as the growth of the physical plant, or the success of an athletic team, are either visible to the public or receive wide notice in the communication media. Almost behind the scenes, however, innovations and adjustments occur which affect the traditions, the operation, and the program of the school. Many such changes have been effected at Wesleyan in recent years.

In 1958 the president of the college was authorized to enter into agreement with the Saga Food Service to operate the dining halls and food servicing. In 1960 this agreement was expanded to include the snack bar in the student center.

The Board of Trustees authorized in 1958 the preparation of a new history of the college to be completed for the Diamond Jubilee celebration.

A new Service Center was established in 1958 in the basement of the Lynch-Raine Administration Building. The center processes all college mimeographing and auto-typing, and dispenses all office supplies. A telecord dictating service was located in the center and made available to all faculty members.

During the summer of 1959 all books in the field of Bible and religion were moved to the Methodist Room in the Annie Merner Pfeiffer Library to establish a new library of religion under the direction of Dr. Kenneth M. Plummer. This centralized the college holdings in the field with the collection of the West Virginia Methodist Historical Society. From this collection a circulating library for the ministers of the West Virginia Annual Conference was established. Dr. Plummer was also assigned the responsibility of preparing the new history of Wesleyan.

President Martin noted in 1959 the creation of a Committee on Wills and Estates under the direction of Mr. James I. Ling. A list of eighteen hundred prospects who might make Wesleyan a beneficiary was compiled. Two hundred seventy-five Methodist attorneys and trust officers were enlisted to serve on the committee.

With the untimely death of Dean Arthur Schoolcraft in 1959, Dr. Orlo Strunk, Jr., assistant dean and associate professor of psychology, was elected to the office of dean of the college. Dean Strunk, a native of Pennsylvania and a veteran of World War II, did his undergraduate work at Wesleyan. He returned to Wesleyan after earning the S.T.B. and the Ph.D. degrees at Boston University.

The office of dean and registrar were separated also in 1959, and Mr. Patton L. Nickell, Jr., a Wesleyan graduate, became registrar.

In March 1959, President Martin was authorized by the Board of Trustees to appoint a committee of two representatives from the Board of Trustees, the West Virginia Annual Conference Board of Education, the Pittsburgh Annual Conference and the faculty to consider the development of a graduate school of religion at Wesleyan. While no specific action was taken to establish such a school, the concern reflected in the proposal and the deliberations of the committee have been incorporated in President Martin's proposal for the reorganization of the total educational program at Wesleyan.

121

During the commencement in May 1961, a group of twenty Wesleyan alumni who were graduates of fifty years or more organized an "Emeritus Club." The purpose of the club is to encourage alumni of fifty years or more to return to the college each year for commencement, and to hold meetings of their own annually in the interests both of the members and of the college. The organization of this group came largely out of the efforts of the late Mr. Clyde O. Law who became its first president.

The school year 1960-61 saw the inauguration of two lectureships, the Windover-Hills Lectureship in Religion with Dr. Nels F. S. Ferre of Andover-Newton School of Theology as lecturer, and the Arthur A. Schoolcraft Lectureship with Dr. J. Edward Dirks of Yale University as lecturer.

Four new religious groups developed on campus during 1960-61 under the auspices of the Methodist Student Movement; the Hour of Power, a meditation group; the Caroleers, a choral group interested in religious music; the Dramateers, a dramatic group interested in religious drama; and the Wesley Weds, a fellowship for married students.

The office of Director of Evaluation Services was established in 1960-61.

A Christian Arts Festival, underwritten by the General Board of Education of The Methodist Church for the first two years was held April 26-28, 1962. The festival, an annual event, features a showing of original paintings in Christian art.

A seminar on alcohol studies was jointly sponsored by the college and the Board of Christian Social Concerns of The Methodist Church in March 1962. A similar seminar was held again in 1963-64. A featured lecturer both years was Dr. Albion R. King internationally recognized as an authority in the field of alcohol studies and a former member of the faculty at Wesleyan.

The Board of Trustees voted in 1963 to give a 50 per cent reduction in tuition to children of all Methodist ministers serving under episcopal appointment within the bounds of the West Virginia and Western Pennsylvania Conferences of The Methodist Church, to the children of ministers of the Central Jurisdiction where it overlapped these conferences, and to the children of all Methodist ministers under special appointment who were serving within the bounds of these conferences at the time of their appointment.

Several notable achievements in athletics have been recorded in recent years by Wesleyan teams. In each successive year from 1957 through 1960, under the coaching of Frank Ellis, the basketball teams were West Virginia Conference champions, NAIA District 28 champions, and each year won two games in the NAIA Tournament at Kansas City, Missouri. In 1961 the football team coached by Sam Ross won the state championship and the West Virginia Bowl championship. From 1954 through 1958, and again in 1960 and 1964, the track team won the West Virginia Intercollegiate Athletic Conference championship. WVIAC championships were won also by the tennis teams of 1962 and 1964, coached by Dave Reemsnyder, and by the baseball teams of 1955 and 1956, coached by Frank Ellis. Wesleyan has competed in golf since 1955, but there have been no outstanding teams to date. The track team coached by Bill Pugh won the state championship in 1964.

During the same period a number of Wesleyan athletes have received recognition. In football Cliff Judy, Jim Hawkins, Dean Patenaude and Bill Wood were named to the WVIAC all-star conference team and the Methodist all-American team. In basketball Gary Hess, Jim MacDonald and Ken Remley were selected for the WVIAC all-conference team and the NAIA all-American team; Bill Smith was elected to the NAIA all-tourney team and the NAIA all-American second team. Ken Remley was listed also in *Who's Who in Small College Basketball*. In baseball John Elmer Houdashelt was named on the WVIAC all-conference team.

VI

WESLEYAN, WHAT KIND OF COLLEGE?

In a formal sense the Christian college has been defined as an institution of higher learning under ecclesiastical or denominational control or auspices. In a deeper sense, however, the Christian college has claimed for itself educational dimensions and, hopefully, distinctive characteristics which give it a unique place in the educational scene. The necessity of defining its distinctiveness has constituted a crisis with which the Christian college has been confronted in America.

A prior crisis which the Christian college faced was economic in nature. During the mid-nineteenth century the mortality rate among such schools was high. The struggle of the Methodists to found and maintain an educational institution in West Virginia, and the history of Wesleyan itself in attempting to achieve financial stability illustrate the pressure which for many years has kept church-related colleges in a state of economic uncertainty.

The problem of adequate financial support is by no means a negligible problem today, but some of the pressure has been eased by growing enrollments and increasing concern for the support of higher education. The imperative facing the Christian college now is that of defining its conception of itself and its role in higher education. It must do this in the face of the criticism that though at one time church-related colleges played a significant role in American education, they no longer do so. Questions are being asked. Are there any distinctive and unique facets of the life and work of the Christian college which make its survival and growth imperative? If there are not, will the Christian college cease to exist, not in the sense of going out of business, but in the sense that it will become an institution which makes no claim to being Christian or distinctive?

Within the last decade serious thought has been given by educators within and without the Christian college as to the distinctive and creative role it can play in higher education. This is not to say that the question had not been previously raised. It is to say that recently educators generally have been pondering the adequacy of the philosophy of education under which they have been operating. In the face of the increasing secularization of western culture the Christian community has become involved deeply in this appraisal, especially at the point of examining the relationship of the church and the Christian faith to higher education.

Out of the probing which has been taking place the ideal shape of a Christian college has begun to emerge.[1]

It is generally agreed that a college, whether it be a private or a church-related institution, has two primary functions. First, it should offer a curriculum of sufficient depth to provide the basic knowledge and intellectual skills in the various fields of learning to equip the graduate to live in a swiftly changing world. Second, it should provide the basic education required by an increasing number of students to continue their education either in a graduate or professional school or through self-study.

The Christian college must first strive to be a good college in this sense. It cannot excuse academic incompetence in the name of piety, and it must be judged by the criteria by which any educational institution is judged. The distinctiveness of the Christian college on this point lies in the fact that it sees its calling to be a good college as a calling under God, and its search for truth is characterized by openness to Christian affirmations about man and the universe.

Those who are attempting to define the unique nature of the Christian college are suggesting that within this context it has several further responsibilities.

The Christian college must assist the student in the integration of his intellectual and emotional forces around an examined and relatively consistent philosophy of life. Obviously, this philosophy of life should be related to the Christian faith. The religious orientation of a college can

---

[1] The writer has compiled the image of the Christian college from a representative sampling of a large body of literature on the subject which has appeared in recent years:

The Christian Scholar, XLI, Autumn, 1958; a special issue devoted to addresses and reports of the Second Quadrennial Convocation on the subject, "The Vocation of the Christian College

George H. Williams, "The Christian College Today."

Jerald C. Brauer, "The Christian College in American Education."

John D. Moseley, "A Fresh Look at the Christian College."

Kathleen Bliss, "Christian College and Contemporary World."

Study Section Reports on The Theological Foundations of the Christian College, The Relation of Church and Campus, The Christian College and the Student's Sense of Vocation, The Christian College and the World Mission of the Church.

Addresses delivered at the 17th Institute of Higher Education of the Board of Education of The Methodist Church, Nashville, Tennessee, July 28-31, 1963:

John Brademas, "The Church-Related College and Present Trends in Education."

Albert E. Burke, "The Multiversity and the Liberal Arts College."

John O. Gross, "Why College?"

Earl J. McGrath, "Are Quality Higher Education and Church-Relatedness Incompatible?"

Orlo Strunk, Jr., "Liberal Arts and the Christian College," The Christian Century, April 18, 1962.

Richard N. Bender, "Marks of the Church College," Trustee, XIX, March, 1965.

be a boon in fulfilling this responsibility in an age in which there is an intensive search for meaning. A traditional concern of the Christian college has been for the relatedness of reason and faith. To fail to assess the significance of faith for the human enterprise is to leave the student a fragmented individual. The Christian liberal arts college, it is affirmed, can provide a unique forum where vigorous search may take place for relationship among ideas and between disciples, between factual evidence and religious insight.

The Christian college, therefore, has a special responsibility to transmit through its academic disciplines the Biblical, historical, theological and ethical content of the Christian heritage. It must relate these to other disciplines. It must avoid a dogmatic or catechetical approach. Its primary function is not to indoctrinate but to examine and inquire.

The Christian college also has the responsibility of providing a regular and genuine experience of worship in which the total community participates. A word of warning is issued generally on this point. The Christian college cannot contend that it is fulfilling its function as a Christian institution when it includes scholarly study of the Judeo-Christian heritage in its curriculum or when it has a compulsory worship service. The sin of the Christian college has not been failure to provide worship opportunities but rather the failure to provide a relevant academic and community life which offers the kind of setting which nurtures and sustains worship.

With respect to its academic life, the Christian college has a charter of freedom provided by the Gospel with its demand to seek the truth. Obedience to this demand requires openness to formulations of truth from any who undertake with deep seriousness the intellectual inquiry. The Christian college should be, therefore, an independent center of radical criticism covering the whole range of major intellectual, cultural and social concerns, including religion. In this venture the Christian college can render a service to the church by preventing its life and faith from becoming stagnant and unrelated to the major contemporary movements of thought and life. It can provide the occasions for conversation between those who are not actively identified with the church and those who are members of the Christian community.

Those who are concerned about the academic approach of the Christian college suggest that one of the chief difficulties of this kind of college springs not from its religious ties or orientation but from a confused or false conception of its proper sphere of inqury. Instead of providing a full and integrated liberal arts education, the Christian college projects the image of the university with its mutiform professional programs and its research specialists. The opinion of many educators who attempt to spell out the distinct and creative contribution which the Christian college can make in the educational scene today is that it should concentrate on a liberal arts education as the basis of all sound education including graduate and professional training. The experts decry the fact that the Christian college has tried and is still trying to be all things to all men not in order to witness to the vitality of the faith, but in order to keep the doors open and the school solvent. This criticism is directed especially at purely vocational courses. While not denying that some liberal values can be found in vocational subjects properly taught, there is considerable agreement that the liberal arts college should eliminate them. It is argued that the Christian college should concentrate seriously on the humanities, the arts, the social sciences and the natural sciences in humanizing, civilizing and emancipating the student. The liberal arts taught within the framework of a community informed by the Christian faith can bring discipline and openness to the student. Such an academic program can prepare the student to live within a framework of life which has wholeness, and in which life is understood as a calling or vocation from God. It can prepare the student not simply to adjust to the world as it is, but to remake it.

The Christian college in order to fulfill its mandate to pursue the truth must partake of some of the essential qualities of the religious fellowship of the church itself. That is, the Christian college must become a community of acceptance and forgiveness and not just a community of scholars in the usual sense. As a community of scholars it should provide through its faculty an example of high intellectual competence and expect of its students a life of intellectual achievement and excitement. It must provide an atmosphere which shows free and open respect for ideas. However, the academic atmosphere can breed intellectual prima donnas; it provides a soil in which the sins of pride, envy, ambition and self-centeredness can and do flourish, in which there is a tendency to judge all learning by one field, in which criticisms are avoided which often ought to be faced. The Christian college can make a unique contribution in this area, inasmuch as it should be a Christian community in which all members are free to be themselves, and to accept and forgive others as they have been accepted and forgiven. Acceptance and forgiveness do not imply mere tolerance or indifference. They do imply a community in which the tensions, conflict and unrest which inevitably develop out of genuine inquiry and provocative scholarship do not produce division, but develop persons who can be their honest, best selves. They do imply an academic environment in which persons can be released from the fears, compulsions and defensiveness which block full human and intellectual development.

Even the non-Christian scholar, it is suggested, should be able to find a congenial place within the community of a Christian college, since the Christian doctrine of creation affirms that we are members one of another, a fact which holds regardless of the presence or absence of religious belief.

There is a second sense in which a Christian college should partake of the qualities of the church. It should exhibit a distinctly Christian ethos. It should recognize the distinctiveness of the individual and produce individuals who have a genuine concern for the welfare of others. It should be in a position to enroll risk cases and the promising student handicapped by inequalities of race and economic hardship. While the Christian college is neither a reformatory nor a camp-meeting nor a finishing school, it should seek to foster attitudes and values indigenous to the Judeo-Christian heritage as well as the most creative aspects of the cutural heritage. It should foster a quality of recreational and social life which is enlightened, consistent with the nature of the institution and satisfying to the entire person. It should encourage student Christian organizations which contribute to mature participation in the life of the church, the major concerns of national and world student Christian movements, and in significant social action. It should function in a climate of decision making in which trustees, administrators and faculty members understand and implement in every phase of the institution's life the ethical imperatives of the Judeo-Christian heritage.

While partaking of the qualities of the church, the Christian college must distinguish itself from the church. While operating from the perspective of the Christian faith, it must be aware always that the liberal arts have an autonomy and integrity of their own, and they must not be used as a pulpit from which to preach the Christian faith. The Christian college will have the concern of the church for evangelism, but its method of evangelism is limited by its nature as a college committed to the search for truth from every source. Therefore, it cannot emphasize disproportionately nor neglect the Christian view of truth. It must leave the student free, under God, to choose. The evangelistic methods open to the Christian college consist of the general spirit and atmosphere of the college, the quality and Christian life of its faculty and administrators, the concern and witness provided by extra-curricular Christian organizations. On a deeper level, the evangelistic thrust arises out of the extent to which the pursuit of knowledge is felt to be a Christian vocation, the work to which God has called this particular community. Hopefully, the Christian college should provide the church with graduates who have an examined and matured faith which has been related to other perspectives and to the major, persistent questions of life, death and purpose.

The faculty of a Christian college usually elicits special comment by those concerned for the ideal pattern of such an institution. In addition to providing a faculty of scholars, the Christian college must provide a climate conducive to professional growth. Even though salaries are not up to the standard of institutions not related to the church, the Christian college can attract scholars for whom sound scholarship, dedication to liberal arts education and a program directed toward a well-defined end may take priority over salary schedules. Nevertheless, in order to remain competitive in the rapidly expanding field of higher education, the Christian colleges are faced with the necessity of increasing salaries.

There is general agreement that the Christian college should require of its faculty, in addition to scholarly competency, acknowledged Christian character, respect for the spiritual ideals of the institution. This does not mean that faculty members are to be required to subscribe to a formal or doctrinaire religious position. It does mean that the Christian college can ask that the faculty and other members of the community respect the basis from which it operates, and that the Christian concern of the college be taken seriously as deserving proper consideration, exploration and expression in life.

An obvious area in which the Christian college has a distinct contribution to make is the service it can render the church in the training of clergy, missionaries and Christian educators. In addition, it can provide leadership in many aspects of the work of the church in the world from its reservoir of scholarly Christian teachers and administrators.

What kind of college is West Virginia Wesleyan College? How has it defined its role as a Christian college of liberal arts? In the attempt to answer this question, Wesleyan, in company with many similar schools,

129

has grappled over the years with the question of: Precisely what aspects or qualities of the institution make it a distinctive educational institution? How should Wesleyan implement its desire to be both a sound community of learning and a school for Christians in its total program?

Before the school was established, the founding fathers clearly indicated their intention that it would be a co-educational school, owned and operated by The Methodist Church, though in no sense a sectarian institution. The school would provide a high order of instruction, but it would also assume a high degree of responsibility for the inculcation in its students of manners and morals, and the duty of loving and serving God and of accepting Jesus Christ as the Savior of the soul. The school would be not only a help to learning but also a fountain of piety. Echoing this characterization, the seminary catalogue for 1890 affirmed that "it will be the aim of the institution, not simply to produce scholars, but to develop character, to promote Christian culture and the truest refinement of thought and conduct."

The school placed itself on record as desiring to furnish a thorough and systematic education to any young person wishing an education. It cautioned, however, that none but persons of good moral character need apply for admission. "While we seek to help every student to form right habits of life, the incorrigibles are not wanted; the seminary is not a reform school." Good health, good habits, ordinary intelligence and a resolute will to get an education were the primary qualifications for admission. Discipline, it was announced, would be kind but firm. The faculty would endeavor to look after the welfare of students and supply, as far as possible, the lack of parental control and counsel. The ideal sought for each student was the highest degree of self-control. One way in which the school articulated its objectives was succinctly stated:

> Our purpose is to make the moral and religious life of the school such that parents may feel that their sons and daughters will be safe under its influence.

From 1890 to approximately 1928, Wesleyan's attempt to fulfill its function as a Christian institution included the determination to lead uncommitted students to a definite decision for Christ. Reflecting this evangelistic thrust, the catalogue for 1900-01 affirmed that the college should be as much and more a center of Christian work and influence, as much an agency of evangelism, as the church itself. For the first thirty years of the life of the school, yearly evangelistic meetings or revivals

130

were held, aimed at securing the conversion of the unconverted. The school took pride in the fact that its faculty was committed to this revival effort, that its leading students were committed Christians, and that among students it was respectable and popular to be a Christian. Late in the twenties the notice of yearly revival meetings disappeared. Concern for the religious welfare of the student continued but was stated in a different way:

> Recognizing that the foundation and inspiration of the noblest character is Jesus Christ, the quiet but constant influence of the college tends to lead the student to a life of definite allegiance and loyalty to Him. During the year special meetings are held in the interest of student religious life. These meetings treat the problem of the student from a sane, practical standpoint, endeavoring to lay the emphasis on the essential Christian spiritual values.

The desire to be a Christian institution is one thing; implementing this aim is quite another. Those who have been responsible for guiding the program of the institution have always been aware of this fact, and they have frequently analyzed the difficulties of making and keeping a college Christian. It has been suggested, for example, that compulsory chapel often fails as a means of making a profound religious emphasis. Other stumbling blocks have included lack of real backing by the church, financial distress, failure of those entrusted with responsibility for the school to understand its Christian orientation, and the imperfections and frailties of human nature. A past president of Wesleyan once lamented that Christian colleges had been called unchristian because they had given aid to athletes, granted too many scholarships, been too aggressive in collecting student accounts; because dancing had been permitted or not permitted; because discipline had been too lax or too strict.

Whatever Wesleyan's record has been in achieving its ideals, it must be said that those who have administered the affairs of the school have exhibited all the arts and zeal of the Puritan in self-analysis and introspection. Dr. Roy McCuskey noted that the Christian college must be constantly evaluating itself in order to approximate as closely as possible its standard. Is it Christian in teaching, in business relations, in the example set by personnel, in social attitudes, in forms of recreation and play? It must be concerned with refining the varied interpretations held by students, clergy, faculty and trustees of "just what is Christian" in all phases of college life. A further dimension of the problem has been identified by Dr. Stanley H. Martin when he notes the need for defining the difference between the church and the college, for seeing the Christian college with its roots and fulfillment in the Christian community but with a primary and specialized focus on learning. A school like Wesleyan must always be engaged in dialogue over the problem of how it can be at the same time an outstanding liberal arts college and an effective arm of the church. This dialogue takes place at Wesleyan in many forums, structured and unstructured.

Wesleyan has attempted to implement its Christian emphasis in a number of ways. It has always been assumed that a prime requisite is a faculty whose members are competent scholars in their fields and committed to a Christian philosophy of life. A resolution was adopted by the Board of Trustees in 1900 affirming "that hereafter no teachers nor assistant teachers shall be employed in the West Virginia Conference Seminary who are not active Christians and members of the church." It has held to this resolution. While the school is Methodist owned, many Protestant denominations have been represented on its faculty.

Wesleyan has emphasized traditionally the personal encounter between faculty member and student as a focal factor in its uniqueness as a Christian institution. Dean Orlo Strunk, in stressing the fact that Wesleyan always has conceived of its function to be teaching, notes that teaching has never been considered as synonymous with classroom instruction. An integral function of the teacher in a Christian community is to be a teacher in and out of the classroom. The close relationship, the personal encounter between members of the staff and the student body, gives substance to Christian concern for the individual, his problems, his abilities, his interests.

From the founding of the school through 1927, all students were required to attend daily chapel, consisting generally of singing, prayer and a short address. These were reduced to three per week in 1928 and to one per week in 1937. The revival meetings of the first three decades gradually gave way to Religious Emphasis Week early in the thirties, and to Christian Emphasis Week in 1951. In addition to these activities, Sunday afternoon study groups during the early years, weekday vesper services, student retreats, prayer groups, required and elective courses in Bible and religion have provided depth to the religious emphasis of the life of the school.

Through the years a number of organizations devoted to a specific religious emphasis have arisen, most of which have served a particular need or have reflected current trends in religious activity on college campuses. These include:

1906-1937, YMCA; 1906-1946, YWCA promoted Bible and Mission study classes, conducted religious services, gave aid to students in securing room and board.

1910-1947 Wesleyan Student Volunteer Band provided study, discussion, and activity for students; promoted interest in foreign missions.

1913-1925 Homiletic Association provided students preparing for the ministry an opportunity to present papers and hear addresses by invited guests.

1926-1928 Ministerial Association patterned on the Homiletic Association; has been revived occasionally, most recently in 1960.

1937-1938 The Lantern aimed at promoting creative fellowship and recreation, discussion of the problems of youth and major contemporary problems such as war and peace, race prejudice, prohibition.

1947-1952 Christian Service Fellowship, Student Christian Association.

1951-1952 MYF and several denominational organizations.

1956—Methodist Student Movement.

1957-1960 Hillel Society.

1957—Sigma Theta Epsilon, National organization of Methodist Men.

1958-1959 Methodist Girls Club.

1960—Kappa Phi, National organization of Methodist Girls.

1962—Canterbury Club, Episcopal Students.

1962—Newman Club, Roman Catholic Students.

From the turn of the century down to 1934 the Christian associations sponsored a lecture course of six to eight numbers per year which brought to the campus distinguished lecturers and men of letters.

The attempt has been made through the years to promote the religious emphases on the campus through faculty and trustee committees on religious activities. The Religious Life Council, composed of faculty and students who represent the religious interests of the college community, and the major denominations represented in the student body was organized in 1959 to coordinate the religious life program of the campus.

As a Christian college, with the brand name Methodist, Wesleyan has sought to minister to the needs of The Methodist Church through the variety of services previously noted. The student body has always been largely Methodist. However, the school has never been sectarian either in its teaching or in its recruitment of students. It has operated on the hypothesis that a student body which is interdenominational and inter-faith in character provides the soundest atmosphere for the enrichment and deepening of Christian thought and experience. The late Dean Schoolcraft in discussing the complexion of the student body affirmed that Wesleyan must make room always for all qualified Methodists who seek

133

admission. Beyond that the school must make room always for highly qualified students of every creed, every continent, every color. "We must be as broadly catholic as we aspire to be Christian." Any other policy would be ". . . a reversion to primordial provincialism and prejudice, of the pre-Jonah type, that would utterly disqualify us as Christians, and as participants in building an ever better world order into an ever closer approximation to the Kingdom of God."

Wesleyan's concern to be a Christian college has not preempted the primary reason for its existence, that it is an institution of learning. The school has operated under the assumption that it is fulfilling one of the legitimate and historic functions of the church, that of education. While it has attempted to undergird its total program with a religious emphasis, Wesleyan has based its work on the premise that it would fulfill its function as a Christian institution in the deepest sense by providing its students with the best education possible within the limits set by the personnel, facilities and financial means at its disposal.

Attempts to crystallize the basic philosophy of the school have been numerous. Typical of these are the following statements which represent the spirit of the school midway in her history and as currently defined:

> Nothing is more characteristic of Wesleyan than her insistence upon sound learning being joined to sterling Christian character. . . .
> It is the purpose of West Virginia Wesleyan College to be a Christian College of Liberal Arts in the sense that its total program is directed toward the development of competent, cultured, Christian persons.

The purpose of the institution thus defined is in the nature of broad general objectives. However, as the philosopher A. N. Whitehead has observed, while we think in generalities, we live in particulars. As the school matured and sought to clarify its function, the need for particularizing the generalization became apparent. Since 1950 the college has committed itself to helping each student in the light of his individual needs, abilities and interests to become competent, cultured and Christian by attaining certain specific objectives:

1. Ability and disposition to read the English language with understanding, and to speak and write it correctly and effectively.
2. Ability and disposition to think clearly, objectively, independently, and constructively.
3. Ability and disposition to order one's own life in such fashion as to realize the highest possible degree of health and efficiency of both body and mind.

4. A broad orientation in the liberal arts—some understanding and appreciation of the content and value of the main fields of learning and of the major problems of human life.
5. Sufficient concentration in some field, or fields, to constitute adequate preparation for graduate study or immediate entrance into some well considered vocation. Through its program of testing and guidance the College undertakes to help the student to choose wisely his vocation or profession. Through its instructional program it undertakes to help him acquire the knowledge and develop the skills essential to success in his chosen field.
6. Understanding, appreciation and experience of the Christian religion—development and practice of a Christian philosophy of life.
7. Ability and disposition to be a good citizen—to participate in, and assume leadership in, socially constructive organizations and activities; and to foster extension of democracy and development of a worthy cosmopolitanism.

These objectives, which presently constitute Wesleyan's statement of purpose, have been characterized by President Stanley Martin as a declaration of intent which indicates that the original emphasis of the institution upon scholarship, respect for personality, religious motivation, personal discipline, and a life of service continue to be the guiding principles of the institution.

In this statement of purpose emphasis is laid on broad orientation in liberal arts. A careful analysis of the curricular offerings from 1890 to the present reveals that from its inception Wesleyan has succeeded in basing its total program on a solid core of liberal arts subjects. The curriculum has been organized into the conventional divisions and departments of the traditional liberal arts college.

However, Wesleyan is not and never has been strictly a liberal arts college. The school, responsive to both public need and public demands, has offered a variety of non-liberal arts programs.

The non-liberal arts courses now organized in the Division of Applied Arts and Sciences point up a problem with which schools like Wesleyan have wrestled in the attempt to provide a broad, liberal arts training and, at the same time, prepare students for a vocation or profession. Wesleyan has held to the conviction that her primary thrust is not in the vocational field, but that the school has a responsibility to its students to prepare them to earn a livelihood. Nevertheless, it has tried to keep work in the applied arts and sciences within certain limits. From its inception, Wesleyan has required all students to complete a program of courses covering all areas of liberal arts subjects. This work is currently structured in the General Education requirements covering a two-year period.

During the depression of the thirties, when competition for students was especially acute, President McCuskey warned against the attempt to attract students by proliferating vocational courses:

> Our work is not primarily in the vocational field. We cannot build up a competing university by expanding our curriculum to take in all sorts of technical training. . . . We cannot run here and there, and proclaim the kingdom of heaven in big enrollments, in diversified, sprawled-out courses in everything under the sun from the classics to tonsorial art and beauty culture.

The ideal which appears to have guided Wesleyan has sought to combine training for a useful career with an education in the liberal arts and the development of Christian character. Apparently it has had to resist the temptation to venture too far afield in the area of vocational training, and, in some respects, has engaged in this kind of education with some misgivings. In recent years, various proposals have come from within the college community for reorganizing the whole program on a solid liberal arts basis. The suggestion has been made by the North Central Association that Wesleyan should evaluate the offerings organized in the Division of Applied Arts and Sciences to determine if they meet needs among its constituents, and to ascertain if the vocational majors represented there are needed in addition to its satisfactory liberal arts curriculum. Without prejudicing the issue, it can be said that these vocational concerns have been at the heart of Wesleyan's educational program for her seventy-five years of existence. On this point Wesleyan falls short of the ideal pattern of the Christian college devoted exclusively to liberal arts education. There is no evidence that Wesleyan will alter the course established at its founding. Dean Orlo Strunk, Jr., has argued cogently for the continuation of the educational program which Wesleyan and many similar schools offers. Aside from the extensive and radical revamping of the total program of the school which the initiation of a purely liberal arts program would require, there could arise a real problem at the point of recruiting students. The possibility of a lack of interest in a liberal arts emphasis on the part of vocation minded young people today cannot be ignored. On this point, it can be noted that during the thirties Wesleyan discontinued the Department of Business Administration as part of the retrenchment of its program. Within a few years it had to be restored because of popular demand. Further, asserts Dean Strunk, it would be a tragedy if large numbers of teachers, business administrators and nurses were to seek out less liberal fields of study and never be exposed to the Christian ethos and the broad spectrum of liberal arts inquiry which one hopes prevails in most Christian colleges. The idea that liberal arts courses are more highly esteemed by the Lord than vocational courses, or the assumption that the Christian college cannot teach non-liberal arts subjects within the context of a truly liberal approach are both judged to be highly questionable.

At Wesleyan there has been a proliferation of scientific and professional organizations which have served to stimulate academic interest and intellectual curiosity beyond the classroom. For the first twenty or thirty years of the life of the school, this end was served in large measure by the literary societies. These eventually gave way to groups which represented specific academic interests. The following roster of groups reflects this development:

> Benzene Ring (Chemistry), 1925- .
> Biology Club, 1926; replaced by Nucleus Club, 1936-37; replaced by Beta Beta Beta, 1947- .
> Wesleyan Chamber of Commerce (Business), 1927-31.
> Philosophical Club (Philosophy), 1928; replaced by Pi Epsilon Theta, 1949- .
> Pi Kappa Delta (Forensics), 1928-58.
> International Relations Club (Political Science), 1931- .
> Haught Literary Society (English), 1937- .
> Home Economics Club (Home Economics), 1938; replaced by Betty Lamp Club, 1943- .
> Sigma Alpha Sigma (Honorary Scholastic), 1939-50; two divisions: Beta for Women, Alpha for Men.
> Olympic Club (Athletics), 1936-47.
> Women's Athletic Association, 1940- .
> Future Teachers of America (Education), 1942- .
> Alpha Psi Omega (Dramatic Arts), 1943- .
> Delta Psi Kappa (Athletics for Women), 1949- .
> West Virginia Wesleyan Psychology Club, 1951- .
> Sociology Club, 1954- .
> Student Art Guild, 1959-60; Kappa Pi, 1962- .
> Music Educators National Conference, 1960- .
> Honorary Business Society, 1962- .
> S.N.E.A. (Education), 1962- .
> Debate Club (Speech), 1962- .
> Torch and Tassel (Honorary Scholastic and Activities for Junior and Senior Men), 1962; replaced by Omicron Delta Kappa, 1963- .
> American Guild of Organists, 1962- .
> Blackstone Law Club, 1963- .
> Psi Chi (Psychology Honorary), 1963- .
> Soquinta (Honorary Sophomore Scholastic), 1964- .
> Sigma Eta Sigma (Honorary Scholastic for Women), 1965- .

137

All the ingredients on the level of curricular offerings which make for intellectual pursuit and of a structure of worship and study which make for an understanding of the meaning of the Christian faith are present in the Wesleyan milieu. Are these elements welded together into a community where learning is considered a Christian vocation? Does the college community possess the essential characteristics of the church, those of acceptance and forgiveness? Does it use fully its charter of freedom to pursue the truth from whatever source it comes? Are students given the opportunities to develop fully their potential?

One can suggest a number of facets of the life and work of Wesleyan which point to the answer to these questions.

Wesleyan subscribes to the statement on academic freedom of the American Association of University Professors. There are no impediments to the discussion of any issue or the teaching of any idea beyond the requirements of good taste, intellectual honesty, and the adequate presentation of all sides of any question. There is a feeling on the part of some members of the community that the general pattern of thought which pervades the staff is too homogeneous, and that points of view which are at variance with the general pattern could be represented more adequately by persons committed to them.

There is concern for the development of the whole person. This concern is evidenced in the attempt to provide an educational program which is balanced, to offer ample outlet for creative involvement in extracurricular activities, to insure at least a minimal participation in physical exercise and sports, and to share in the experience of worship on a community level and in small groups. Through testing, counseling and personal encounter the attempt is made to help the individual find himself, to discover his interest and develop it. However, with the rapid increase in recent years of the size of the student body, difficulty has been experienced in keeping the personal touch, in which Wesleyan has taken pride, as vital as the members of the community would like it to be. In order to maintain this traditional emphasis, the administration has made every effort to augment the faculty with teachers who are in sympathy with the aims and ideals of the institution.

There has been recognition also of the lack of a structured interdisciplinary approach, of opportunity for independent study by students, and of an articulated philosophy or purpose which would give unity and direction to the work of the community. In a number of fields attempts

138

are being made to overcome the lack of interdisciplinary study and of independent study.

Some doubts have been expressed as to whether Wesleyan has achieved a genuine Christian educational community. The Survey Report of the University Senate and the Board of Education of The Methodist Church took note of the extensive efforts of the school to provide the soil out of which such a community might grow. Nevertheless, the heterogeneous nature of the student body, and the considerable number of students from differing backgrounds, pursuing goals with no special religious motivation or orientation, was singled out as having produced a situation in which many students feel that the Wesleyan emphasis on religion is somewhat extreme.

Further, the report noted, despite many factors contributing to effective religious cultivation, religion, for the most part, appeared to be understood as connoting certain kinds of formal observances, on or off campus. That there may be religious commitment to truth, to intellectual workmanship, to scholarly achievement, and to vocational fulfillment appeared to the committee not to be very widely held.

One distinguishing characteristic of Wesleyan's approach to its total task, especially in recent years, has been its viability. Increasing emphasis has been laid on experimentation, on finding ways to improve what is being done, on developing an educational program which will keep Wesleyan in the vanguard of the finest liberal arts institutions. Plans have been proposed by several members of the faculty for a total reorganization of the educational program.

A new approach to Wesleyan's total educational program, entitled "An Expanding Purpose," which incorporated suggestions made by these several plans, was presented to the Board of Trustees by President Martin in the spring of 1964. Among the concerns motivating the proposal was the fact, previously noted, that Wesleyan's curriculum is traditional, and that no major changes have been made over the years. Further, even though the objectives of the institution have been clearly stated and partially realized, there has been no conscious effort to implement a specific purpose in recent years.

Aside from these needs in Wesleyan's own program, several forces at work in the general educational picture underscore the need for change. Chief among these are the growing emphasis on professional training and a deeping concern for liberal learning. An effective plan of education,

Dr. Martin noted, must take cognizance of both of these concerns. Wesleyan must train not only technicians but also persons of social conscience, aesthetic and moral principles.

The new approach proposed a hard core of liberal arts studies to be required of all students during their first two years at Wesleyan. Since Wesleyan is a "Christian college," the core program would be strongly oriented toward Christian values. This emphasis would constitute a coordinating thread throughout the student's years at Wesleyan. The closing two or three years of study would be professional or pre-professional in one of eight separate schools of specialized training.

The content of the hard core of liberal arts study was left open for further exploration, but the suggestion was made that it might well center about great ideas, great books, or great principles with a preference for those theologically or religiously oriented.

The eight proposed schools of specialized training are: School of Religion and Humanities, School of Business Administration, School of Education, School of Music and Art, School of Physical Education, School of Social Sciences, School of Nursing, and School of Sciences. Each school would be organized with its own dean, faculty and advisory council. Hopefully, the advisory councils would be composed of national authorities in each discipline and would work with the deans and staff giving professional direction and insight. The schools would not be considered separate entities but would be integrated with and based on the core of liberal arts studies.

Summer programs would be provided for each of the student's years at Wesleyan including the summer prior to matriculation. Before registering for the freshman year each prospective student would be required to master a list of required readings designed to effect the transition from high school to college and lay the groundwork for the first year of study. If necessary, the incoming student would participate in a remedial institute designed to remove limitations and correct deficiencies. A similar program is projected for the summer following the freshman year.

Each degree candidate would be expected to spend the second summer abroad with one of eight tours visiting centers associated with the technical or professional focus of each of the eight schools. Each tour would be planned as a learning experience by a professor who would conduct the tour.

The student's third summer would be devoted to a practicum in his professional field. Under the close supervision of the college and the cooperating agencies, the practicum would be planned as a period of testing and evaluation as the student moves into his fourth year. The fourth year would involve a limited number of formal class situations and would stress senior seminars, honors work and independent study. A comprehensive examination and a senior thesis would complete the required work.

The projection of a Master's Degree in the proposed plan represents perhaps its most unique feature, according to Dr. Martin. Students averaging a grade of "B" or better after four years and three summers of study would be eligible for an M.A. degree. Students maintaining an average of "B" or less could complete work for the M.A. by attending Wesleyan for a fifth year or by transferring to an affiliated university.

An integral part of the graduation requirement for each student would be the completion of a basic course or program of churchmanship and active participation in some creative community project. This program, aimed at developing qualities of churchmanship and citizenship, would be under the supervision of a Director of Community Service and Churchmanship who would initiate projects with municipal and county authorities and church leaders.

Since in the context of modern education good teaching involves sound research, the plan proposes that a basic research project involving both faculty and students should be in process at all times in each of the eight schools. Projects would be correlated by a Campus Director of Research working in cooperation with supervisory faculty members. Pilot studies in each school would be designed to evaluate methods of teaching. Such studies would be under the direction of a Director of Special Instruction and would be analyzed by the Director of Evaluation.

A projected enrollment of 1500 students would require an estimated minimum of 100 faculty members to sustain the program. Fifty per cent of these should have their doctorates with the balance pursuing graduate study toward doctorates. Faculty members would be required, at the expense of the school, to spend a full summer away in study every fifth year in order to keep abreast of method and content in each area of study. Full professors would give lectures. Associate and assistant professors, instructors and teaching fellows would conduct seminars. Teaching fellows would be students who had completed four years at Wesleyan and were candidates for the M.A. degree. Tutors from the senior class

141

would be assigned to the various dormitories. Each year a scholar of national repute would be invited to the campus to spend a year in residence as visiting professor in some aspect of the core of liberal studies. He would be responsible also for the upper level courses in the area of his specialization.

Under the plan three vice-presidents would be appointed, one in charge of academic affairs, one in charge of financial matters, and one in charge of development. The deans of the eight schools would form a University Senate and function under the supervision and direction of the academic vice-president.

President Martin's suggestion that international study and travel should be a part of the educational experience at Wesleyan was picked up by Professor Duncan Williams, graduate of Christ Church College, Oxford University, England, and presently a member of the faculty of the English Department at Wesleyan. Professor Williams suggested that a branch institution might be established by buying or renting a suitable country property near Oxford, England, where up to a hundred students might study each year. The stimulus of sustained foreign contact could be achieved without a language barrier, the way would be opened for further travels in Europe, and a situation would be created in which the total learning process might be approached in a more integrated way.

This anticipated approach to learning was, again, a move in a direction pointed out in President Martin's "Expanding Purpose," but initiated from within the faculty and channeled through the Committee on International Studies formed in January 1965. The committee was to make policy suggestions and to serve a coordinating function for several aspects of international study and travel which were entering various stages of planning. It tackled the "England plan" as its first project. In addition to exploring the possibilities for housing the branch institution, the committee constructed a curriculum divided into two lecture courses with seminar and tutorial work taken in conjunction with each course. The lecture courses serve an integrating function, with the seminars and tutorials encouraging concentrated study in special areas of importance and interest. One lecture course centers around an historical approach from the Renaissance through the nineteenth century, while the other course concentrates on contemporary systems and problems.

These proposals for giving Wesleyan a fresh approach to its total educational program are under discussion. Whatever their future may be, it can be said that a creative ferment is at work in the community, that not only will the face of Wesleyan change as campus and facilities expand, but that the next decade is almost certain to see significant developments in its academic life. It may be said also that these developments will reflect the ideal of Wesleyan to develop competent, cultured, Christian persons.

APPENDIX

LIST OF PRESIDENTS
OF THE
BOARD OF TRUSTEES

Samuel Woods 1887-1897
H. C. McWhorter 1897-1913
Charles W. Lynch 1913-1926
Samuel V. Woods 1926-1928
John Raine 1928-1933
Clyde O. Law 1933-1956
E. Ray Jones 1956-1959
Myron B. Hymes 1959-

LIST OF PRESIDENTS

Bennett W. Hutchinson 1890-1898
Frank B. Trotter (Acting) 1898
Simon L. Boyers 1898-1900
John Wier 1900-1907
Carl G. Doney 1907-1915
Thomas W. Haught (Acting) 1913-1914
Wallace B. Fleming 1915-1922
Thomas W. Haught (Acting) 1922-1923
Elmer Guy Cutshall 1923-1925
Thomas W. Haught (Acting) 1925-1926
Homer E. Wark 1926-1931
Roy McCuskey 1931-1941
Wallace B. Fleming (Acting) 1941-1942
Joseph Warren Broyles 1942-1945
Arthur Allen Schoolcraft (Acting) 1945-1946
William John Scarborough 1946-1956
Arthur Allen Schoolcraft (Acting) 1956-1957
Stanley Hubert Martin 1957-

LIST OF DEANS

Frank B. Trotter 1890-1907
William A. Haggerty 1907-1909
Thomas W. Haught 1909-1929
Oscar Doane Lambert 1929-1944
Arthur Allen Schoolcraft 1944-1959
Orlo Strunk, Jr. 1959-

INDEX

147